Group Experience

So Long, Insecurity

LEADER'S GUIDE

BETH MOORE

Tyndale House Publishers, Inc., Carol Stream, Illinois 60188

Visit Tyndale's exciting website at www.tyndale.com.

Visit Living Proof's website at www.LProof.org.

TYNDALE and Tyndale's quill logo are registered trademarks of Tyndale House Publishers, Inc.

So Long, Insecurity Group Experience Leader's Guide

Designed by Jacqueline L. Nuñez

Published in association with Yates & Yates (www.yates2.com).

ISBN 978-1-4143-4991-6

Printed in the United States of America

17 16 15 14 13 12 11

7 6 5 4 3 2

Contents

In the months after *So Long, Insecurity* was published, I started an online discussion group about the book on my blog. I was stunned by the response. Hundreds of women logged on to share their thoughts each week, and who knows how many more read along without commenting. My staff and I were blown away by the women's heartfelt, thoughtful comments and their desire for encouragement and accountability as they worked through the material. It was clear that insecurity was a topic that deeply touched my readers. Not only that, but it was a topic women wanted to discuss together, in a community.

That's why I've created this group-experience guide—to provide a way for you to meet with other women and together get the most from this material. I've highlighted the book's key points, included additional Scripture to shed light on the security only God can give us, and provided questions to get the discussion rolling. At the end of each chapter you'll also find an "On Your Own" section, which includes suggested activities to help you cement the material you covered that week.

Our walks with Christ are individual, but they're also something we can share together. My hope is that your discussion group will become a safe, loving community where you can build relationships, care for each other, hold each other accountable, confess your failings, share your successes, and lift each other up in prayer.

God can do miraculous things! As you begin this group experience, may you come fully believing that the Lord can work in your life, heal your insecurities, and make you whole. I'm excited to see what He will do.

SUGGESTIONS FOR LEADERS

Thank you for being a part of the *So Long, Insecurity* group experience. I am excited to see how God will work, and I'm so grateful to you for being willing to facilitate a group of women. Here is some information that will help you in leading your group.

TIME FRAME

The material in the group experience can be adapted for a variety of settings. Each week's study will probably work best if you have about an hour and a half for discussion. However, it can also work in a shorter format, such as a Sunday school class. The study is designed to be done over ten weeks.

GROUP SIZE

If possible, I encourage you to keep the groups to between eight and twelve women. A larger group can be intimidating for some women, and a smaller group may be too small if some members cannot attend every session.

GETTING THROUGH THE MATERIAL

Depending on how long your sessions are and how talkative your members are, you may not have time to cover all the material. As the discussion flows, keep an eye on the time and be prepared to skip over some sections as needed. I have highlighted the questions that are most important in each week. (Look for questions marked with an asterisk.) If you have to skip over a significant amount of content, encourage the women in your group to read over those questions on their own.

EACH WEEK

- Before your group meets, pray that God will direct your discussion in a meaningful way.

- Each week's study is based on one or more chapters from *So Long, Insecurity.* Encourage the women in your group to read those chapters before you meet. This will not always be possible for everyone, so excerpts have been included from the relevant chapters to set the stage for the discussion questions.

- Warm-up questions are included for each week. Use your discretion on these; if the group is comfortable together after the first few weeks, the questions may seem unnecessary, and you may prefer to jump into the content right away.

- It may be helpful to read aloud the sections entitled "A Word from Beth" and the transitional paragraphs throughout the group experience guide.

- Encourage each participant to bring a Bible. The sections called "In the Light of the Word" typically include several passages to be read aloud and discussed.

- It's helpful to include a short time at the beginning or end of each session for women to share prayer requests. Encourage your group to pray for each other during the week.

- Each session ends with an "On Your Own" section, where I offer suggestions for activities each woman can do individually. Encourage those in your group to choose one or more of these to complete each week.

- Follow up with women who miss a session. Let them know that the group missed them, and encourage them to attend the following week.

TONE OF THE GROUP

It's probably no surprise that a discussion group on insecurity is going to attract women who struggle with insecurity! Do your best to ensure that your group is a supportive place where each woman can share her own fears and the things that trigger them. As a leader, try to set the tone for your group. Encourage participants to agree that there will be no belittling, no one-upmanship, and no gossiping about other members of the group. As you hear about others' fears and hurt places, strive to respond with compassion. Speak truth and strength to each other. Be mirrors of God's love and grace. Ask the Holy Spirit to help your group accomplish this.

DEALING WITH PROBLEMS

Insecurity is a highly personal topic, and because of that, many of the discussion questions relate to the participants' own experiences. Some women will be reluctant to share about their fears and struggles, and other women may be too open. As a leader, you can address this in a few different ways:

- If a discussion is getting bogged down because the same people share at length each time a question touches on personal experiences, you may decide to skip some of the more personal questions and move on to others that are more objective.

- Be sensitive to the less talkative women in your group. Draw them out when you sense they have something to say.

- If necessary, speak privately with women who are dominating the conversation. Express your love for them and your appreciation for their participation, and then ask for their help in making sure everyone in the group gets a chance to participate.

- If a woman is sharing so many personal details that you think she may regret it later, gently step in and redirect the conversation. Similarly, if one of your group members has significant struggles that are beyond the group's ability to address, privately express your support and suggest that she meet with the pastor or a professional Christian counselor for assistance.

I pray God's blessings on you as you begin this group experience!

—*Beth Moore*

Insecurity: A Bad Friend

> *Blessed are those who trust in the L*ORD
> *and have made the L*ORD *their hope and confidence.*
> *They are like trees planted along a riverbank,*
> *with roots that reach deep into the water.*
> *Such trees are not bothered by the heat*
> *or worried by long months of drought.*
> *Their leaves stay green,*
> *and they never stop producing fruit.*

JEREMIAH 17:7-8, NLT

WARM-UP

Welcome your group to the first meeting. You might want to say something like this: "We're blessed to be in this unique group of women. Each of us is valued and dearly loved by God. Each of us is a mix of vulnerability and confidence, weakness and strength. Together we're about to embark on several weeks of learning and growing. My hope is that we'll start building a foundation of trust and love by getting to know a little about each other over the next ten weeks."

Before you dive into the study, have women pair up, chat for a few minutes to find out about each other, and then introduce each other to the whole group. Along with the person's name, it's fun to throw in a few interesting details, such as the person's best-loved restaurant, favorite pastime, or hidden talent.

Once everyone has been introduced, transition into the core material—why you're really here. Raise these questions for discussion:

THIS WEEK'S FOCUS
To grasp how pervasive insecurity is among women, and to get a glimpse of what security in God might look like.

BEFORE YOU MEET
Before your group meets, read the introduction and chapter 1 of *So Long, Insecurity.* As you read, highlight or underline parts that jump out to you. What rings true to you? What surprises you? What seems most challenging?

1

*What prompted you to join this group? Why do you want to read and discuss this book? What do you hope to gain by the end of this journey?

_____

_____

_____

_____

_____

What will help you get the most out of this experience? What do you need from the group?

_____

_____

_____

_____

_____

A WORD FROM BETH

{Note to the leader: You might want to read the following aloud to the group.}

I'm thrilled that you're starting this discussion about *So Long, Insecurity*. Walking through the door for the first session might be the hardest thing you do today. I've heard so many stories from women who bought the hardcover book and immediately had to remove the jacket because they were embarrassed to carry around a book about insecurity! I'm right there with you. It takes a lot of guts to participate in a discussion that will require some vulnerability, and I'm so proud of all of you for starting this journey. I wish I could look each of you in the eyes and tell you that it will be so worth it.

What's our goal for these next ten weeks? When I was in Birmingham, Alabama, on a book tour promoting *So Long, Insecurity*, a cameraman from a local television station asked me that very question. I'll tell you what I told him: the goal is for an insecure woman to open the book and a secure woman to close it. Nothing less than that. Humanly speaking, fat chance. But what if, somewhere in these pages and through our discussions, we hear God speaking instead? Ah, then, for those willing to believe what He says, fat chances lose their weight and real changes take their place. We're not just looking to talk about a book here, sisters. We're looking to discover the kind of soul-deep security that stands fast in the floodwaters of this image-saturated society. It is time for a change.

DIGGING IN

This week we'll start with an overview. How common is insecurity, anyway? How does it affect us and our relationships with God?

In the introduction I write honestly about insecurity in my life:

> My entire life story grows like a wild shoot from the thorny soil of insecurity. Every fear I've faced, every addiction I've nursed, every disastrous relationship and idiotic decision I've made has wormed its way out of that sorrowfully fertile ground. Through the power and grace of God, I've dealt with so many side effects of it, but oddly, until now, I've somehow overlooked its primary source. . . . Glance around you. Do you see another woman? She probably shares that battle too. Regardless of our professions, credentials, or possessions, the vast majority of us are swimming in a sea of insecurity and trying our best to hide behind our goggles. (pp. xi, xiii)

Then in chapter 1 I talk about how insecurity affects all of us as women:

> I'm feeling ticked for the whole mess of us born with a pair of X chromosomes. My whole ministry life is lived out in the blessed chaos of a female cornucopia. I've been looking at our gender through the lens of Scripture for twenty-five solid years, and I have pondered over us, taken up for us, laid into us, deliberated over us, prayed about us, lost sleep because of us, cried for us, laughed my head off at us, and gotten offended for us—and by us—more times than I can count. And after a quarter of a century surrounded by girls ranging all the way from kindergarteners to those resting on pale pink liners inside caskets, I've come to this loving conclusion: we need help. *I need help.* Something more than what we're getting. . . . I hear echoes of fear and desperation from women day in and day out—even if they're doing their best to muffle the sound with their Coach bags. Oh, who am I kidding? I hear reverberations from my own heart more times than I want to admit. I keep trying to stifle it, but it won't shut up. Something's wrong with us for us to value ourselves so little. Our culture has thrown us under the bus. We have a fissure down the spine of our souls, and boy, does it need fixing. (pp. 2, 4)

*How pervasive is insecurity among women? Are there some women who seem to get off the hook when it comes to insecurity, or do you think it's something we all grapple with?

_____

_____

_____

_____

_____

When was the last time you came face-to-face with our gender's struggle with insecurity? Have you ever felt angry about the extent to which insecurity affects women?

_____

_____

_____

_____

_____

What helps you feel secure? When in your life have you felt the most secure?

_____

_____

_____

_____

_____

In chapter 1, I recall hearing a sermon about what a woman needs from a man. As the pastor talked about how a husband needs to affirm his wife's beauty and desirability, I wondered,

> "What if no one tells us that? Can we still find a way to be okay? . . . Is there no validation for our womanhood apart from a man?" . . .
>
> Men are not our problem; it's what we are trying to get from them that messes us up. Nothing is more baffling than our attempt to derive our womanhood from our men. We use guys like mirrors to see if we're valuable. Beautiful. Desirable. Worthy of notice. Viable. (pp. 5, 7)

Why do we do this? At times we really seem to think our worth depends on qualities we have little control over, such as appearance or personality. We think someone else's opinion matters that much. We give other people so much power over us, and we need to get it back.

As a father has compassion on his children, so the LORD has compassion on those who fear him; for he knows how we are formed, he remembers that we are dust. (Psalm 103:13-14)

*In our culture, how much weight do women place on male validation? Share a specific example of how you see this reflected in today's movies, television, or music.

_____

_____

_____

_____

_____

What problems might result from this dependence on the approval of men?

_____

_____

_____

_____

_____

IN THE LIGHT OF THE WORD

Now that we have an idea how widespread insecurity is, let's find a little hope. It's easy to look around at our culture and at our own lives and see what we *don't* want—a sense of self-worth that balances precariously on someone else's opinion and leaves us fragile, overly sensitive, and unable to look beyond ourselves. But what's the alternative? What can we hope for? Here's my answer from chapter 1:

I want some soul-deep security drawn from a source that never runs dry and never disparages us for requiring it. We need a place we can go when, as much as we loathe it, we *are* needy and hysterical. I don't know about you, but I need someone who will love me when I hate myself. And yes, someone who will love me again and again until I kiss this terrestrial sod good-bye. (p. 10)

Where can we get that kind of security?

We'll talk a lot more about this in the weeks to come, but for now, let's look at a few Scripture passages that point the way to the ultimate answer.

*Read Jeremiah 17:7-8 out loud. According to this passage, what are the characteristics of a secure person? Where does security have its roots?

_____
_____
_____
_____
_____

What does it mean to make the Lord your hope and confidence? Can you think of a time when you were able to do this? What happened?

_____
_____
_____
_____
_____

*Read Psalm 103:13-18 out loud. Which phrases in the passage highlight how short life on earth is? Which words remind us of God's eternal nature?

_____

_____

_____

_____

With vivid language, the psalmist reminds us that everything on this earth will fade away or fail us. We know that nothing material will last for eternity, but sometimes we forget that things on earth will fall apart even in our lifetimes. When was the last time you held on to a relationship, a bank account, or a role you thought was secure—only to see it crumble? The stock market crashes, people let us down, our appearance changes, our kids grow up. We know we shouldn't expect to find security from men, our dress size, our IQ, or a showpiece house, but we're so desperate that we try to grab it anywhere we can. Unfortunately, looking for security from an unsteady source only makes us more likely to fall.

This isn't meant to be a downer, because the truth is, when everything else fails, we're pointed to the one thing that never fails. The one thing that lasts forever—the one thing that can give us a secure foundation—is the rock that is our Lord.

*The Lord created us and knows how frail and shaky our lives are. Still, what is His response, according to Psalm 103? What might that tell us about how He views us when we struggle with insecurity?

_____

_____

_____

Two key words in this passage are compassion *and* love. *The Lord knows how frail we are, how emotionally fragile our insecurities make us—and He loves us with an everlasting love anyway. With that kind of love as an anchor, you've got to know there's help for us on the horizon.*

WRAP-UP

I hope you come away from this week with a taste of what it might mean to find true security. I also hope you are beginning to feel more comfortable with each other as you undertake this journey to wholeness. Next week we'll look at the definition of insecurity. We'll put a face to this enemy of ours and try to understand why he can be so hard to shake.

Community is built through caring and prayer. As time permits, share prayer requests within the group and pray for one another. Encourage group members to write down the requests so you can pray throughout the week.

ON YOUR OWN

- Write a journal entry describing this present season of your life and why you've chosen to read this book. What do you want to get out of it? How do you want to be changed at the end of the journey? If you're comfortable doing so, consider writing the entry in the form of a prayer.
- As you write, think about how you can reach your goal. What do you need to do to get the most out of this experience? (Journal regularly? Read the chapters each week? Pray about your struggles in a focused way? Meet with an accountability partner to keep you on track?) Whatever it is, commit to doing it. Remember, the goal is for you to close this book a secure woman. That's worth some effort!

WEEK TWO

How Insecurity Affects Us

We are God's masterpiece. He has created us anew in Christ Jesus, so we can do the good things he planned for us long ago.

EPHESIANS 2:10, NLT

WARM-UP

Go around the room and have each woman choose one of the following questions to answer briefly:

What was your first paying job?

What do you listen to while driving?

When you have an hour or two all to yourself, what do you like to do?

After everyone has had a chance to share, open your discussion time with this question:

What do you think of when you hear "insecure woman"? What stereotypes come to mind?

_____

_____

_____

_____

_____

THIS WEEK'S FOCUS
To begin to understand what insecurity really is and how it hinders us personally.

BEFORE YOU MEET
Before your group meets, read chapters 2 and 3 of *So Long, Insecurity.* As you read, highlight or underline parts that jump out to you. What rings true to you? What surprises you? What seems most challenging?

A WORD FROM BETH

{Note to the leader: You might want to read the following aloud to the group.}

Forgive me for sounding like a commercial for laundry detergent, but the lid of my washing machine has guidelines for getting tough stains out of clothes. You know—blood, grease, chocolate, ink, grass. I guess it's good the instructions are there, because the procedure for each stain is different and I can never remember what to do right off the top of my head. The point is that knowing what caused the stain is critical. If you don't know what it is, it's a lot harder to get out.

Maybe this is a corny analogy, but here's the tie-in: before we can get serious about cutting insecurity out of our lives, we have to understand exactly what it is. That's why we're going to spend time today trying to define it. I hope you'll have some good discussion about what insecurity means and the ways it can raise its ugly head in our lives.

We'll also talk about the concept of false positives and the way we tend to envy others who have what we think would make us secure. Let's be honest: there may be envy here in this very room today. Let me encourage you with all that's in me not to let that envy get in the way of the support a group like this can offer. Let's ask God to give us eyes to see each other clearly and to give us hearts that overflow with compassion rather than comparison. May your time of discussion be blessed!

DIGGING IN

How do we know if we have a problem with insecurity? Here's what I say in chapter 2:

> We all have insecurities. They piggyback on the vulnerability inherent in our humanity. The question is whether or not our insecurities are substantial enough to hurt, limit, or even distract us from profound effectiveness or fulfillment of purpose. Are they cheating us of the

powerful and abundant life Jesus flagrantly promised? Do they nip at our heels all the way from the driveway to the workplace? Scripture claims that believers in Christ are enormously gifted people. Are our insecurities snuffing the Spirit until our gifts, for all practical purposes, are largely unproductive or, at the very least, tentative? Maybe you can answer each of those questions with an honest no. The only reason I'm bothering to write a book instead of leading a small group, however, is because I believe if you can, you'd be in the vast minority. I'm convinced that many women—if not most—have enough insecurity to hinder them. (pp. 15–16)

*Share a specific time in your past when insecurity kept you from doing something you wanted to do or stopped you from using your gifts. How does it hinder you today?

_____

_____

_____

_____

_____

Before we go much further, we need to develop a working definition of insecurity. How would you define *insecurity* in a word or a brief phrase?

_____

_____

_____

_____

My one-word take on it is self-sabotage. *Also, I believe that our discussion on insecurity should be framed by two words:* chronic *and* intensity. *These separate the woman mildly hindered by insecurity from the woman paralyzed by it.*

Here's one definition from author Joseph Nowinski, author of *The Tender Heart*:

> Insecurity refers to a profound sense of self-doubt—a deep feeling of uncertainty about our basic worth and our place in the world. Insecurity is associated with chronic self-consciousness, along with a chronic lack of confidence in ourselves and anxiety about our relationships. The insecure man or woman lives in constant fear of rejection and a deep uncertainty about whether his or her own feelings and desires are legitimate. (p. 17)

*What parts of this definition seem accurate? Is there anything about it that surprises you? If you feel comfortable sharing, explain how you fit this description.

_____

_____

_____

_____

_____

Part two of Nowinski's definition centers on insecurity's toll on relationships:

> The insecure person also harbors unrealistic expectations about love and relationships. These expectations, for themselves and for others, are often unconscious. The insecure person creates a situation in which being disappointed and hurt in relationships is almost inevitable. Ironically, although insecure people are easily and frequently hurt, they are usually unaware of how they are unwitting accomplices in creating their own misery. (p. 23)

Think about a few movies or television shows you've seen recently—or even items in the news. Can you find some examples of self-sabotage in relationships?

_____

_____

_____

_____

_____

We now have this light shining in our hearts, but we ourselves are like fragile clay jars containing this great treasure.
(2 Corinthians 4:7, NLT)

What unrealistic expectations have you placed on relationships in the past? How can we become more conscious of our negative patterns in relationships?

_____

_____

_____

_____

_____

In chapter 3 I write about a key concept called the "false positive." It all started with words from a friend of mine:

> "You know, Beth, people who don't know you really well would never be able to imagine that you struggle with insecurity. . . . After all, you're so tiny."
>
> That's when it hit me. Most of us have what I'll call a prominent false positive: *one thing* that we think would make us more secure in *all things*. You want to know how you can pinpoint your own prominent false positive? The thing you tend to associate with security? Think of a person you believe to be secure and determine what earthly thing he or she has that you don't feel like you possess, at least in matching measure. That's liable to be your prominent false positive. (pp. 36–37)

*Look through the list of false positives on page 38. Which ones resonate most with you? Can you identify your false positive—the one thing you think would make you secure?

_____

_____

_____

_____

_____

IN THE LIGHT OF THE WORD

When we face our false positives (and our false assumptions) head-on, we start to realize how deceptive insecurity is. Because the truth is that nothing on earth—not a great job, a wonderful husband, a beautiful face, or a fit body—has the power to make us secure. Our insecurity is too deep to be fixed so easily. But though we may be mired in self-consciousness and unhealthy patterns, we are not hopeless causes. In fact, if we have Christ within us, we have the promise that one day we will become like Him.

*Read Romans 8:9. What hope does this verse offer?

_____

_____

_____

_____

_____

*Read 2 Corinthians 4:7. What words does this verse use to describe Christ living within us? How should this transform the way we view ourselves?

_____

_____

_____

_____

_____

When we lose sight of the treasure God has placed inside each of us, our viewpoint gets skewed. Not only do we see ourselves as worth less than we are, but we even start to think God might not know what He's doing. In chapter 2 I share how my own insecurities affect my view of God:

> This morning I went on a walk to listen to praise music on my iPod and hold the themes of this book out before God in hopes that He would speak to my heart. He spoke, all right. I realized that maybe I don't just doubt myself. Maybe I subconsciously doubt God for using me. Let me be frank: if I were God, I wouldn't have given me a second look. I constantly feel unqualified, inadequate, and out of my league. I realized this morning that I not only lack security, I also lack faith. I don't just doubt myself, I also doubt God *about* myself. It was a revelation to me. Almost a horror. I wonder if you can relate. (p. 18)

Read Psalm 139:1-4, 13-14. What does this passage reveal about how well God knows us? How does He view us, even with that full knowledge?

_____

_____

_____

_____

_____

*Read Ephesians 2:10. How are believers described in this verse? What impact should this truth make on how you view yourself and how you live your life?

_____

_____

_____

_____

_____

I praise you because
I am fearfully and
wonderfully made; your
works are wonderful,
I know that full well.
(Psalm 139:14)

In different translations of this verse we are described as God's workmanship or His handiwork—or even His masterpiece! Bask in that for a moment. Some of us can get hung up on the "good works" mentioned later in the verse because we start thinking that maybe we're not qualified or capable enough to pull those off. But guess what? Our Lord not only created us perfectly for that purpose, but He equips us to do the things He has called us to. He has even prepared specific assignments for us!

It's almost like a Sunday school teacher who helps her preschool students make a craft. She doesn't set them loose with art supplies and expect them to come away with a painting that rivals the Mona Lisa. *Instead, she chooses a project within their capabilities, prepares the supplies ahead of time, walks the kids through each step, and provides hands-on help when necessary. Those young students are set up for success. How much more will the God who created us—and who views us as the pinnacle of His creation—lovingly help us fulfill His purpose for us?*

*Read 1 Peter 2:9-10. How are believers described in this passage? What is our purpose?

_____

_____

_____

_____

_____

No matter what our situation, my friends, we can declare God's praises! It doesn't require skill or beauty or poise or even confidence to do that. All it requires is a grateful heart.

How is it that we somehow believe we know ourselves better than God knows us? He tells us that we are chosen, called, and equipped for work in His Kingdom—but we think He doesn't realize just how flawed we are. Sisters, let's put those lies aside. Believe these words from Scripture! Trust them. The Author of them is faithful and true. His voice is the one we need to hear.

WRAP-UP

To finish your discussion, have someone read this challenge out loud (from the end of chapter 3):

> That, beloved, is our challenge. To let the healthy, utterly whole, and completely secure part of us increasingly overtake our earthen vessels until it drives our every emotion, reaction, and relationship. When we allow God's truth to eclipse every false positive and let our eyes spring open to the treasure we *have,* there in His glorious reflection we'll also see the treasure we *are.* And the beauty of the Lord our God will be upon us. (p. 43)

As time permits, ask women to share their needs, and take time to pray for each other.

ON YOUR OWN

- Think of one of the women who sat near you in this week's session. Over the next week, pray the wrap-up challenge for her, lifting her up before the Lord and asking Him to work in her heart for this glorious purpose. Pray it for yourself as well.
- Reread Psalm 139, Ephesians 2:10, and 1 Peter 2:9-10 each day this week. Let the truths of God's Word penetrate your mind and heart.
- In your journal, write some reflections about this question: what barriers does insecurity place on you that you want to be free from?

Good Company

*I sought the LORD, and he answered me; he delivered
me from all my fears.*

PSALM 34:4

WARM-UP

*Go around the room and have each woman choose one of the
following questions to answer briefly:*

What would be your ideal vacation?
What's one of your favorite holiday traditions?
What song have you had stuck in your head today?

*After everyone has had a chance to share, open your discussion
time by reviewing the challenge you talked about last week.*

Last week we ended by reading the challenge from chapter 3—
a challenge to let God's truth about ourselves take center stage
and remind us of the treasure we *have* in Christ and the treasure
we *are* in Christ.

***How has this challenge affected you in the past week?
Have you noticed any changes in the way you think or
react to things that would typically trigger your insecurity?**

_____

_____

_____

_____

_____

THIS WEEK'S FOCUS

To understand that insecurity touches everyone—even people who are greatly used by God.

BEFORE YOU MEET

Before your group meets, read chapter 4 of *So Long, Insecurity*. As you read, highlight or underline parts that jump out to you. What rings true to you? What surprises you? What seems most challenging?

A WORD FROM BETH

{Note to the leader: You might want to read the following aloud to the group.}

If you're ever tempted to think that the people we read about in the Old and New Testaments had picture-perfect lives, think again. Some of these folks make us look like paragons of emotional wellness! We'll look at some of these people in all their lack of splendor and realize they're pretty much just like us. We'll also discover that God still considered these weak, insecure, fearful people to be usable for His purposes. In fact, some of them, like Moses and Paul, are considered giants of the faith! Praise the Lord for His ability to redeem even our weaknesses for His glory.

DIGGING IN

Several biblical characters are mentioned in this chapter: Eve (see Genesis 3), Sarai and Hagar (see Genesis 16), Rachel and Leah (see Genesis 29:31–30:24), Moses (see Exodus 3–4:17), Saul (see 1 Samuel 10:9-27), and Paul (see 2 Corinthians 11:5-6 and 12:11).

As you read the accounts of insecurity in this chapter, which of these biblical characters do you most identify with? Which ones have your sympathy, and why?

_____

_____

_____

_____

*Is it a new idea for you to interpret these people's actions in the light of insecurity? How does it change your perception of these men and women?

_____

_____

_____

_____

_____

Early in this chapter I retell the story of Sarai and Hagar—an infertile wife and an all-too-fertile concubine. It was Sarai's brilliant idea to have Hagar sleep with her husband, Abram, to produce the heir she was unable to conceive. But when the plan worked and Hagar actually became pregnant, things fell apart fast. Hagar despised Sarai, Sarai "mistreated" Hagar (which in all likelihood meant physical abuse), and Hagar fled into the desert.

> We naturally despise people whose company we are forced to share if we feel largely threatened by them.
> _Threat._ That single word captures one of the most powerful drivers of insecurity. More often than not, if we're willing to make the connection, we can trace feelings of insecurity to a perceived threat, especially when it comes in a sudden rush.
> What are we afraid of?
> Who are we afraid of?
> What are we afraid of losing?
> Why are we afraid of being displaced? (p. 48)

Think of a recent situation when you felt insecure or jealous. Can you trace your feelings to something you perceived as a threat? If you feel comfortable, share your experience with a partner or with the group.

_____

_____

_____

_____

"My grace is all you need. My power works best in weakness." So now I am glad to boast about my weaknesses, so that the power of Christ can work through me. (2 Corinthians 12:9, NLT)

What are some of the common fears that fuel insecurity? When you feel insecure, how might it help to stop and ask yourself these four questions from the excerpt above?

_____

_____

_____

_____

Sometimes we are rational enough to realize that what we fear is unlikely to come to pass. When that's the case, we can talk ourselves down from crazy, insecurity-fueled behavior. But the truth is that some fears are valid. Sometimes your husband really is desiring someone else, your best friend really is giving you the cold shoulder, or your boss really did give you a bad performance review. What happens then?

My suggestion is this: even when fears are founded and threats are real and we are about to be swept away in a tidal wave of well-earned insecurity, there is divine power, wisdom, and clarity of thought to be found. The person who responds with strength instead of hysteria at a time like that may be a stranger to you right now, but finding that person is precisely what we are doing here. (p. 49)

*How do you react to valid threats or fears? When these fears prompt intense feelings of insecurity, what tools could you use to deal with them?

_____

_____

_____

_____

_____

A bit later in the chapter we see another example of jealousy: Saul. Ever heard of imposter syndrome? That's when you feel that, although everyone else may see you as competent and qualified for whatever position you're in, you know better. You assume that if other people knew you the way you know yourself, they would agree that you're just not good enough. King Saul was a poster child for imposter syndrome. Not only was he tall, dark, and handsome, but he was chosen by God to be king. Yet from his first public act (hiding among the baggage) to some of his worst later moments (trying to kill the young hero David) he lived and breathed insecurity. And unfortunately, we can relate.

Have you ever experienced imposter syndrome? What brought it on, and how did you deal with it?

_____

_____

_____

_____

Insecurity lives in constant terror of loss. Insecure people are always afraid that something or somebody is going to be taken from them. Saul feared the loss of power and admiration, and he quickly ascertained that David would be the one to try to take them from him. He didn't quite get that God alone was in charge of his destiny and the only one who could jar that crown off his head. (p. 54)

*Insecurity is driven by the fear of loss. What do you most fear losing, and how does that fuel your insecurities?
This is a very personal question, but it's an important one. Assure group members that they won't be forced to share if they don't feel comfortable answering out loud, but encourage them to reflect on their answer and jot down their thoughts in private.

_____

_____

_____

_____

_____

What role do you believe God plays in handling your life and your future? What impact does that have on how you deal with your fears?

_____

_____

_____

_____

_____

IN THE LIGHT OF THE WORD

As we move into a deeper look at Scripture, let's take one more cue from King Saul:

[Saul] let his emotions get so out of control that his insecurity morphed into complete instability. It happens. Interestingly, Saul had moments of emotional sobriety when he knew how far left he'd gone and even wept with regret over his actions toward David. Nevertheless, he refused to call out to God for deliverance from his own unhealthy emotions. (p. 55)

Can God even deliver us from our emotions? You bet!

*Read Psalm 34:1-4. Why is the writer of this psalm praising God?

_____

_____

_____

_____

_____

*When was a time you experienced God delivering you— setting you free—from your fears? If you feel comfortable, share with the group.

_____

_____

_____

_____

_____

Let's be clear here: Insecurity tempts us to wallow in our unhealthy emotions. It tells us that there's no way out, and it calls us deeper and deeper into the pit of fear, jealousy, and self-loathing. But God's Word says there is a way out. He is the way out! Read 1 Corinthians 10:13. What does God promise in this passage?

_____

_____

_____

_____

_____

When has the Lord provided a way out of temptation for you? What do you think would happen if you prayed for Him to make a pathway out of your insecurity?

_____

_____

_____

_____

_____

Now let's take a look at the life of Paul. He is an example of hope for us, because he was transformed through Christ.

*Read Acts 7:54–8:3, which shows what Paul's life was like before he encountered Christ. After committing his life to Christ, what might Paul have felt insecure about in regard to his past?

_____

_____

_____

_____

_____

Saul had persecuted Christians directly; he had stood by at Stephen's execution; he had not followed Jesus during His ministry on earth.

Can you imagine going through life as a missionary when at any moment you might come face-to-face with one of the believers you had persecuted? "Hey, Paul—nice sermon. I haven't seen you since that time you threw me in jail." Nothing like being reminded of your sin. Or what about those who surely discounted Paul's ministry, even though he had a clear call from God, because he didn't actually know Jesus when He was on earth? No wonder Paul comes across as insecure at times!

But here's the thing: Jesus Christ was conforming Paul to His image, just as He's conforming you and me if we've made a commitment to Him and if we're letting Him work. In his second letter to the Corinthians, Paul goes on at length, telling the church all the things he could boast about on a human level—his Jewish pedigree, his education in the Law, his visions and revelations from the Lord, his hard work, and the suffering he endured because he preached the gospel. But then, with almost shocking honesty, he writes about his weakness.

*Read 2 Corinthians 12:6-10. What does it mean to boast about our weaknesses? In what way are we strong when we are weak?

_____

_____

_____

_____

_____

*Can you think of a time in your life when Christ's grace was sufficient for you? What impact would it have on our sense of security if we truly grasped Christ's sufficiency in our weakness?

_____

_____

_____

_____

_____

I'm pretty sure that Paul's transformation to security was a gradual thing. Just like all of us, he probably took two steps forward and one step back, over and over. But don't be fooled: that's still progress! Every time God teaches us to let go of our egos, our pride, and our constant comparisons with others

Be still, and know that I am God; I will be exalted among the nations, I will be exalted in the earth. (Psalm 46:10)

and replace them with gratitude for His grace, we're moving forward. When we can stop trying to impress others with our accomplishments and instead let them see our true selves—warts and all—we've taken a step toward realizing that our true value doesn't rest on our own strength but on Christ's.

Read Psalm 46:10. Do you ever feel like you're in a battle, constantly striving to look right, dress right, act right? What would it look like to be still—to be free from all that? How might God free you?

_____

_____

_____

_____

_____

The New American Standard Bible *phrases the verse this way: "Cease striving and know that I am God." Many other versions begin, "Be still." Encourage people with different translations to read the verse aloud.*

WRAP-UP

Let's close with this quote from page 57:

> The fact that the inspiration of the Holy Spirit on the pages of Scripture is not dampened by the insecurities of those God chose to pen it is perhaps the greatest testimony to its incomparable potency. After the likes of Adam, Eve, Abraham, Sarah, Hagar, Leah, Rachel, Saul, the woman at the well, the super-apostles, and Paul, surely we can breathe a sigh of relief that we are not alone in our struggles. Human flesh and blood have no weakness so strong that God's strength is made weak.

Praise the Lord for this word of hope! As you pray for each other today, take time to ask God to reassure each of you of His sufficient grace. His strength is strong enough for all our weaknesses.

As time permits, ask women to share their needs, and take time to pray for each other.

ON YOUR OWN

- In a journal, consider the threats you face that trigger insecurity in you. What are you afraid of losing, and how does that fear affect your thoughts and actions? As you write, ask God to reveal the truth about these threats. If they are overblown, ask Him to give you clarity to see them as they are. If they are real, ask for the strength to deal with them with His help.

- Write 2 Corinthians 12:9 on an index card and put it on your mirror, in your car, on the refrigerator, or somewhere you'll see it each day. Pray that God would help you realize that His strength can shine through your weakness. Remember that you are precious and usable to Him.

Digging Deep

THIS WEEK'S FOCUS
To discover the origins
of our insecurities.

*Let your roots grow down into [Christ Jesus], and let
your lives be built on him. Then your faith will grow
strong in the truth you were taught, and you will overflow
with thankfulness.*

COLOSSIANS 2:7, NLT

BEFORE YOU MEET
Before your group
meets, read chapters 5
and 6 of *So Long,
Insecurity*. As you read,
highlight or underline
parts that jump out to
you. What rings true
to you? What surprises
you? What seems most
challenging?

WARM-UP

*Go around the room and have each woman choose one of the
following questions to answer briefly:*

When you were a kid, what was your favorite food?

*What was the last book you read, and what did you enjoy
about it?*

Who is your favorite movie character, and why?

*After everyone has had a chance to share, open your discussion
time with this question:*

**Have you ever done something you knew was silly (like
repark your daughter's car in the school parking lot), but
you did it anyway to prevent embarrassment for yourself
or for someone you love?**

_____

_____

_____

_____

_____

A WORD FROM BETH

{Note to the leader: You might want to read the following aloud to the group.}

The chapters you'll be discussing today lay some important groundwork for the rest of the book because they prompt us to discover the origins of our insecurity. It's been dogging many of us our whole lives, and it's time to figure out where it's coming from!

Let's be honest: some of us find great satisfaction in looking back on our lives and figuring out how we became who we are. We're the ones who can trace our dislike of lima beans to a specific day in October 1995, or our fear of public speaking to a comment someone made to us in kindergarten. But for others of us, this process may be really tough. Trust me, I know that dredging up old memories can be painful. Maybe you think it's a waste of time to look back at things you can't change. You'd like to stop thinking about the problem and move on to the solutions already! If you're in that second group, bear with me for a few chapters. We will get to ways to deal with our insecurity, but first it's critical that we understand some of the causes. No, we can't change what has already happened. (If we could, I'd be giving that magic eraser a big workout!) But we can recognize it, acknowledge it, deal with it, and *then* move on.

One other thing before you start this discussion: this may be a tough week for some of the sisters in your group. Talking about the root causes of insecurity in your life with other women may seem vulnerable and even terrifying. I hope you know that this is a safe group. I pray that all of you will be especially tender toward each other this week, respecting privacy when it's needed but encouraging sharing when that would bring healing. Some of you may not feel comfortable discussing the deepest roots of your insecurity, and that's okay. I encourage you to think through the questions later, either in your journal or one-on-one with a friend.

The questions in today's session may raise some serious issues. Keep in mind that the group is meant to provide love and support— but it's not the place for someone to share lots of details about past abuse or other difficult past situations. You could say something like this to the group: "Today we'll keep the discussion a little more general. If you need to deal in more detail with junk from your past, I encourage you to first get alone with the Lord to pour out your heart to Him. Then, if needed, seek a believing friend or a professional counselor who can help you process it."

DIGGING IN

{Note to the leader: This chapter contains a lot of information, so you may need to skip a few questions and highlight the topics that are most relevant for your group.}

Let's start by listing the roots of insecurity as described in chapters 5 and 6:

- Instability in the home (including various types of abuse, divorce, substance abuse by a parent, mental or physical illness in the home, financial instability)
- Significant loss (of a person, a home, a relationship)
- Rejection (from a parent, friend, spouse, child, boyfriend)
- Dramatic change (accident, financial crisis, even positive changes like a move or a new baby)
- Personal limitations (learning disability, physical handicap, scar, acne)
- Personal disposition and temperament
- Our culture and the pressure it puts on women to be young and beautiful
- Pride

*Some of these roots of insecurity may seem like no-brainers, while others may be less obvious. Do any items on this list surprise you? Which of them do you most relate to?

_____

_____

_____

_____

_____

The LORD himself goes before you and will be with you; he will never leave you nor forsake you. Do not be afraid; do not be discouraged. (Deuteronomy 31:8)

We'll start with *instability in the home*. In chapter 5, I write the following:

> At the root of chronic insecurity is often the primal fear that no one will take care of us. Every single thing that underscores that fear is like fertilizer in the soil. And there's nothing that makes a home less stable than abuse. Any kind of abuse—emotional, mental, physical, verbal, or sexual—not only causes immediate effects, it also goes straight to the core of our belief system and parrots our worst nightmares: *I'm on my own. No one will take care of me.* And not only does it teach us that no one is there to take care of us, it also affirms that those who are *supposed to* care will instead harm us. (pp. 65–66)

Did you experience significant instability in your family? If you feel comfortable sharing, briefly describe your situation.

_____

_____

_____

_____

_____

Think about a time in your life when you felt you were on your own, with no one to take care of you. What prompted the feeling? What effect did it have on you?

_____

_____

_____

_____

_____

A significant *loss* in our lives can also be a setup for insecurity. Sometimes loss comes as a result of something major, such as a death or the end of a relationship. But you might also feel the sting from a series of smaller losses—even things other people might not consider a big deal. It's key here not to judge yourself. The reality is that the loss hurt you and had an effect on you. As I say in chapter 5, "If it translated as something huge to your heart, it is huge to God on your behalf" (p. 71).

*What losses—large or small—have played a part in your insecurity? How does it help you to be reminded that God cares about your loss?

_____

_____

_____

_____

_____

Rejection is one of the most common roots of insecurity.

Few forces can catapult a female into a season of insecurity with the swiftness of rejection. . . . Anywhere there is relationship, there is potential for rejection. Mind you, we were created by God precisely for relationship, so disconnection is not the answer. Restoration is. First, however, we need to take a good look at our insecurities and see if they are tied to our perception of a rejection that sent us reeling.

I used the word *perception* because it is entirely possible to perceive that we've been rejected when we haven't. If our hearts are tender or unhealthy enough, we can turn a reasonable boundary into a full-fledged rejection. In other words, we might have wanted *all* the attention of someone who was only willing to give us a significant portion. . . . We can confuse 80 percent reciprocation with 100 percent rejection. (pp. 71–72)

What people or circumstances make you feel rejected? How do you react when you feel this way?

_____

_____

_____

_____

_____

*Our perceptions of rejection are not always accurate, especially when we're already feeling vulnerable. Can you think of a time when you felt rejected, but looking back, you realize that wasn't the person's intention? How can we deal with feelings of rejection in a healthy way—whether the rejection is real or perceived?

_____

_____

_____

_____

_____

Different personalities react differently to rejection. Some of us try harder and harder to be noticed or accepted. (Think of the junior high girls who never give up in their quest to become one of the popular group, no matter how many times they are scorned.) Others of us stop trying immediately and pretend we don't even care. (The junior high equivalent of the loner who keeps to herself rather than risk approaching a group and not being welcomed.) But neither of these extremes is what God wants for us. The only way to work through rejection is to hear what God says about us—that He wants us, loves us, pursues us, and fights for us.

Dramatic change can throw us into a season of insecurity because we feel the world shifting under our feet. Most of us tend to find comfort in stability and sameness. Big changes feel threatening because they throw us into the unknown. The unknown could even be better than our present, but many of us balk because what we know seems safer than what we don't know.

*What big changes have you experienced in your life— good or bad? How have these changes brought up feelings of insecurity?

_____

_____

_____

_____

_____

When it comes to *personal limitations*, "attitude is everything . . . , and the way you view yourself will acutely shape how others view you" (p. 81). In chapter 5 I tell the story of Lee Sizemore, whose physical disability became the catalyst for his vision to produce an amazing number of video-driven Bible courses.

*Share an example of someone you know whose limitations became their freedom. Why do you think this person was able to rise above the limitations? What role did attitude play?

_____

_____

_____

_____

_____

What limitations have played the biggest role in your feelings of insecurity?

_____

_____

_____

_____

_____

In chapter 5 I share about how *personal disposition* can impact our feelings of insecurity. "The more tenderhearted we are, the more vulnerable to insecurity we'll likely be. Some people take things harder and deeper to heart than others" (p. 83).

On a scale of one to ten (ten being very sensitive), how sensitive would you say you are? How have you seen this correlation between sensitivity and insecurity play out in your life?

_____

_____

_____

_____

_____

In chapter 6 I talk about how *our culture* and the media exploit women. Never in history have women been surrounded by so many opportunities to compare themselves (unfavorably) with gorgeous, airbrushed women.

> We no longer feel inferior to ten other women the way our great-grandmothers might have. We feel inferior to thousands, and as a result, we become less and less satisfied with ourselves until much of our lives are lived on the slippery slope of self-loathing. . . .
>
> That's not all. The high premium on youthfulness has skyrocketed to the point that a woman in her midtwenties now fears she's getting old. (pp. 92–93)

I lift up my eyes to the mountains—where does my help come from? My help comes from the LORD, the Maker of heaven and earth. (Psalm 121:1-2)

Give some examples of unrealistic portrayals of women from magazines, television, movies, or books. How do these media portrayals affect your view of yourself? How might they influence other women in your life (daughters, granddaughters, students)?

_____

_____

_____

_____

_____

How can we be discerning consumers of media? Would you ever consider going on a media "fast"? What do you think the results would be?

_____

_____

_____

_____

_____

Pride is another root of insecurity that I address in chapter 6. This might not have come to mind immediately as a root of insecurity, but it's a big one.

> Let's face it. Sometimes people and situations make us feel insecure because they nick our pride, plain and simple. All the blows of life aside and every other root yanked out of the ground, we wrestle with insecurity because we wrestle with pride. . . .
>
> I have come to the conclusion that we have no greater burden in all of life than our own inflated egos. No outside force has the power to betray and mislead us the way our own egos do. Pride talks us out of forgiving and steers us away from risking. Pride cheats us of intimacy, because intimacy requires transparency. Pride is a slave driver like no other, and if it can't drive us to destruction, it will drive us to distraction. (pp. 100–102)

How has pride been a factor in your life? What circumstances cause it to raise its ugly head?

_____

_____

_____

_____

_____

What is the difference between pride and confidence? What role does humility play in true security?

_____

_____

_____

_____

_____

IN THE LIGHT OF THE WORD

So many of the roots of insecurity come from people who let us down and circumstances that disappoint us—families who weren't there for us, losses that took their toll on us, people who rejected us. There's no glossing over the fact that life can be devastatingly difficult. We may feel like we've earned the right to live with hurt and insecurity. But those of us who know Christ possess an infinitely greater right. In Him, we have the right to be free and whole. We have the God-given right to be secure.

Now that we've got a good grip on the things that bog us down as women, we need to immerse ourselves in what can make us truly secure. Through Scripture, I want to remind us just how rock solid our God really is. He is our only real root of security, and He can comfort us through the struggles life presents us.

*Read the following verses: James 1:17; Hebrews 13:8; and Psalm 102:25-27. What do these verses tell you about God's character? How can those truths comfort us in the midst of instability or change?

_____

_____

_____

_____

_____

Read Psalm 121 and Deuteronomy 31:8. What can we learn about God's care for us from these verses? How can this help us as we deal with feelings of rejection or loss?

_____

_____

_____

_____

_____

*Read Romans 8:38-39.

What a powerful passage! Read it out loud and soak in the promises. Does that touch us where we're at or what? Not even our biggest, craziest insecurities or our failures and sins can separate us from the biggest source of security—God Himself.

We've looked at the roots of our insecurity and stared in the face of things that have hurt us. Now let's put those things in their rightful place. They have harmed us, but they cannot injure us in the most significant way. They are incapable of taking us away from the immense, all-encompassing, unbelievable love of God!

*Let's take a moment to personalize the passage from Romans 8. What would you put in that verse? Fill in the blanks with struggles from your own life: "I am convinced that neither _____ nor _____ will be able to separate [me] from the love of God that is in Christ Jesus our Lord."

_____

_____

_____

_____

_____

*Read Colossians 2:7. We've talked about the roots of insecurity. But what does this passage say about the roots of *security*? How can we let our roots grow down into Christ?

_____

_____

_____

_____

_____

WRAP-UP

You may have had a heavy discussion this week, and some members of your group may be dealing with difficult memories. As you finish your session, read the following quote from chapter 5. Encourage group members to sit with their eyes closed and ask God to help them bask in a fresh awareness of His compassion for them in the midst of whatever terrible circumstances they may have endured. After you've finished, move into a time of prayer, lifting up group members' hurts to God and asking Him to comfort and heal them.

[God] does not take lightly that some of us were raised in a veritable madhouse. He does not take lightly that some of us have been mentally berated or physically beaten or sexually abused or simply abandoned. He does not take lightly that some of us are still trying to recover from that midnight phone call. He does not take lightly that some of us were born with legs that don't work. Or eyes that can't see. Or ears that can't hear. He does not take lightly that some of us have endured the cancer treatment of our very own children. He does not take lightly that some of us, Lord help us, have buried our own children.

He knows it's scary to be us.

Son of David, have mercy on us! It's almost too much to bear here at times, Lord. No wonder we're insecure!

The thunder crashes in the heavens, and the earth grows dark in the middle of the afternoon, and a man, beaten to a bloody pulp, cries from a cross between two thieves, "It is finished!" Because He did, one day God will wipe away every tear from the eyes of those who trusted Him, and there will be no more death or mourning or crying or pain, for the old order of things will pass away and all our hardship will be *finished*. (p. 86)

ON YOUR OWN

- This week, reflect on the roots of insecurity you have faced in your life. Ask God for help as you identify two or three that have impacted you the most, and then bring those hurts to the Lord.
- Take note of the ways we are bombarded by the media with pressure about how we should look and act. Find something, such as an article or an advertisement, to share with the group next week.
- Several times this week, read Revelation 21:3-5. Bask in the knowledge that our God cares enough to gently wipe each tear from our eyes. Thank Him that He will make all things—including us!—new and whole and without pain.

Finding Dignity

She is clothed with strength and dignity; she can laugh at the days to come.

PROVERBS 31:25

WARM-UP

{Note to the leader: This week we're covering several chapters of the book. This may seem like a lot of material at first glance, but it will move quickly. Because chapter 7 is made up of readers' examples of insecurity and almost all of chapter 9 is a prayer that women will look at individually, the majority of today's discussion will center on chapter 8. If time allows, you can follow up on discussions you started or questions you didn't have time to cover from last week.}

Go around the room and have each woman choose one of the following questions to answer briefly:
 Who was your favorite elementary school teacher?
 What is your least favorite chore around the house?
 What story in the news has caught your attention this week?

 After everyone has had a chance to share, open your discussion time with this question:

Chapter 7 contains story after story from women who let insecurity get the better of them. Which ones stood out to you, and why? If you're willing, share a time when insecurity made a fool out of you.

_____

_____

_____

_____

_____

THIS WEEK'S FOCUS
To begin to uncover our God-given dignity.

BEFORE YOU MEET
Before your group meets, read chapters 7, 8, and 9 of *So Long, Insecurity*. As you read, highlight or underline parts that jump out to you. What rings true to you? What surprises you? What seems most challenging?

Did anyone find examples this week of ways the media puts pressure on us as women? Would you be willing to share those examples and your reaction to them?

_____

_____

_____

_____

_____

A WORD FROM BETH

{Note to the leader: You might want to read the following aloud to the group.}

Reading the stories in chapter 7 can be painful—not just because we hurt for the women who have had these experiences, but also because most of us can think of more than a few times when insecurity has made us veer over the line into crazy territory ourselves. But the pain is by design. As I wrote on the _So Long, Insecurity_ blog last year, chapter 7 is meant to hammer a point till you're practically screaming, "That's it! I am sick to death of the toll insecurity takes. I'm willing to do what it takes to dump it." If disgust is the motivation that's finally going to get us to change, I'll take it. Are you there yet?

I'm excited about today's discussion because this is the point where the book begins to turn from the problems to the solutions. We won't just be looking at the negatives of insecurity that we want to escape; we'll also be looking at the positives of _security_. Our goal will start coming into focus as we think about what a secure woman looks like. What kind of women are we striving to be? How does a secure woman react to life and the unavoidable triggers of insecurity?

DIGGING IN

Now that we've dealt with all the roots of insecurity, we can move forward. We probably have a good idea *why* we're insecure, whether it's because of one specific root or many intertwined ones. Thanks to chapter 7, we're also well aware of the ridiculous and often destructive things insecurity can make us do—and we want that to stop! Next we will look at the goal: to become a secure woman.

Chapter 8 is centered on Proverbs 31:25 and addresses the worthy goal of dignity.

*What images or people come to mind when you hear the word *dignity*? Who are some women you know who fit this description? Is dignity a characteristic you associate with yourself?

_____

_____

_____

_____

_____

On pages 148–149 I write the following:

> Insecurity is about losing our God-given dignity. . . .
> Our enemy is hoping we'll get caught in a pitiful cycle of reacting to a sudden rush of insecurity with foolishness, feeling even more insecure, acting even more foolish, and then feeling vastly more insecure. He wants us to keep digging ourselves deeper and deeper into a hole until we feel completely stuck in this miserable corkscrew of self-hatred.
>
> Listen carefully to me: we can begin to break this cycle *this very day*. . . . The cycle begins to break when even though we may still *feel* insecure, we make a very deliberate choice to not act on that feeling.

*How have you experienced this cycle? Have you been able to break it in the past? Do you think it's possible to change?

_____

_____

_____

_____

On pages 150–152 I share some of my story about dealing with my insecurity. Healing hasn't happened all at once for me—it has been more of a process. But I know that Christ has the power to set us free from anything—including insecurity. He doesn't want us to stay stuck there; He wants to transform us so we can see the dignity we have in Him. Let's unpack a few of the ideas we can find in the key verse of Proverbs 31:25:

She is clothed with strength and dignity.

On page 155 I write the following:

I have come to a place where I'm willing to be transparent with my insecurity, but I find great relief that human eyes have to see it through the filter— the clothing—of my God-given strength and dignity. I don't have to stand before you or anybody else in total emotional nakedness. I have a scriptural covering that gives me the courage to expose my most personal self. . . . When you and I are triggered to expose the most vulnerable, broken parts of ourselves through a rush of insecurity, we can train ourselves to immediately recite this truth to our souls: "It's okay. I'm completely clothed." And oddly, that very thought all by itself begins the healing. We are not nearly as likely to react with the same level of insecurity when we remember how well covered we are by God.

*What does it mean to be clothed by God? How does this image help you as you think about putting yourself in vulnerable situations—maybe even this discussion group—where you may be revealing your weaknesses?

_____

_____

_____

_____

_____

> Come to me, all you who are weary and burdened, and I will give you rest. (Matthew 11:28)

Proverbs 31:10 is often translated using the phrase "a virtuous woman." But the Hebrew term for *virtuous* is also used to mean "mighty." *Word Biblical Commentary* translates this phrase as "a woman of *valor*." As we see in verse 25, the woman is described as being clothed with *strength*.

What women do you know who demonstrate might, strength, or valor? Can you think of an incident or a season in your own life when those words described you?

_____

_____

_____

_____

_____

Merriam-Webster's dictionary defines *dignity* as "the quality or state of being worthy, honored, or esteemed." Psalm 8:5 says that God "crowned [humans] with glory and honor," and here *honor* is derived from the same Hebrew term that means "dignity." In other words, we are worthy, honored, and esteemed because God gave those qualities to us! We are His prized creation.

When we're faced with insecurity triggers, we can counter these lies with statements of truth. For example,

- God has made me worthy of respect.

51

- I'm completely clothed by God.
- I am strong in Christ.
- What others think of me is less important than what God says is true of me.

*Which of these affirmations would be most helpful for you? How can you be intentional about incorporating them into your thinking? What others can you suggest?

_____
_____
_____
_____
_____

I hope you can internalize the idea that you are worthy of honor and respect. You are clothed with dignity!

The heart of chapter 9 is to give women an opportunity to ask God, in a time of heartfelt, focused prayer, to restore their dignity and deliver them from insecurity. Since the chapter involves personal, one-on-one time with God, most of the content will be addressed in the "On Your Own" section.

Have someone from the group read the following excerpt out loud from pages 162–163:

Hear this at a yell: it is God's will for you to have your dignity and security restored. You don't need to wrestle with this one. You don't need to read six more books. You don't need to ponder the subject matter until your next big disaster. This one is cut and dry. There are plenty of times when the precise will of God on a matter seems legitimately unclear. You may not know whether He's leading you to change jobs, marry a certain guy, or relocate, for instance, but other questions are answered before we ask them. After twenty-five years of study, if I know Genesis from Revelation, I can promise you that God wills for us to walk out the depth and breadth of our lives with dignity and security. Neither God nor you have anything to gain by your persistent insecurity.

When it comes to dignity and security, we have a golden opportunity to know in advance that we are praying the will of God for our lives. And we need to cash in that request posthaste. We can count on the answer being as sure as the appeal. In fact, if you're willing to exercise the kind of boldness that excites the heart of God, you can go right ahead and thank Him in advance because you know that what you've asked is as good as done.

*How can we approach God with a request when we're certain it's in His will? What kind of freedom does this give us?

_____

_____

_____

_____

_____

IN THE LIGHT OF THE WORD

*Read 1 John 5:14-15 and John 15:7. What things can we know absolutely are in God's will? How can you approach God with confidence as you move into this week of targeted prayer?

_____

_____

_____

_____

_____

Another prayer God always answers is a request for Him to root out our pride. We talked earlier about what a big factor pride is in our insecurity. Why? Because a big ego makes us put ourselves front and center. We waste valuable time and energy wondering if we're prettier or smarter or more accomplished than other people around us—and then dealing with the backlash when we come across someone who clearly outranks us in those areas. Everything becomes about *us*, and too often we can't see past ourselves to notice the real hurt and needs around us. If we are willing to humble ourselves, God will help us change that attitude.

*Read Philippians 2:1-4. What does this passage tell us about pride? In practical terms, what does humility look like?

_____

_____

_____

_____

_____

Pride constricts our thinking. Humility expands it. Pride gives us tunnel vision so narrow we can barely see two inches in front of our faces. And, what's worse, it sucks us dry of energy and compassion. Let's be honest: constantly comparing ourselves with others is exhausting. That's why I love this next passage, with an invitation straight from Jesus.

*Read Matthew 11:28-30. What strikes you about Jesus' example of humility? What kind of rest do you think Jesus is talking about here?

_____

_____

_____

_____

_____

Jesus invites us to stop striving so hard. We can stop trying to get God to love us because of the things we do. We can stop seeking other people's approval. We can stop competing in our own internal contests, trying to be the first or the best or the most popular. Those are the things that burden us, that exhaust us. Guess what? We can let them go.

We don't need to hold on to pride. We don't have to compete or compare, because Jesus offers grace and rest when we follow Him. His love is unconditional. The value He places on us as His beloved creation is unconditional. You don't have to earn the right to have respect and dignity—He makes you worthy of it. Praise the Lord!

WRAP-UP

Talk about the prayer in chapter 9 and encourage the women in your group to set aside time with the Lord this week to go through it. With the group, pray about the experiences they will have in the coming week. Ask the Lord to speak to each woman and encourage her in this journey of transformation. You may want to have someone lead the group in the brief prayer below.

Although you will be spending time reflecting on the prayer in chapter 9 on your own, you may want to pray the following prayer (adapted from page 165) as a group:

> Dear God,
> We come to You this moment because we need some things only You can give us. We need restoration, Lord. We need our dignity back. You alone know what insecurity has cost us, what trouble—even torment— it has caused us. . . . We desperately need and want to be delivered from our chronic insecurity. We are ready to discover what it means to be truly secure. Amen.

ON YOUR OWN

Take time this week to pray through the prayer in chapter 9. Whether you read it out loud or write it out, I encourage you to make it personal and real. Pour out your heart to the Lord. And remember that it is His will for you to be secure. He will answer your sincere prayers, and you will start to see changes in the way you view yourself and the world around you. I pray fervently for each one of you that this week may hold the day that you begin to let the Lord transform you. Remember: *She is clothed with strength and dignity.*

Clearing Our Vision

Since we are surrounded by such a great cloud of witnesses,
let us throw off everything that hinders and the sin that so
easily entangles. And let us run with perseverance the race
marked out for us, fixing our eyes on Jesus, the pioneer
and perfecter of faith.

HEBREWS 12:1-2

WARM-UP

Go around the room and have each woman choose one of the
following questions to answer briefly:

What was your favorite class in high school?

Who was your first close childhood friend? What did you
enjoy doing together?

What is something your family enjoys doing together?

After everyone has had a chance to share, open your discussion
time with this question:

*Last week we ended with the challenge to spend time one-
on-one with God, reflecting on the prayers in chapter 9.
Were you able to take time for that this week? If you'd like
to, share something about the experience. Was it meaningful?
awkward? humbling? challenging? encouraging? What did you
take away from your time with the Lord?

_____

_____

_____

_____

_____

THIS WEEK'S FOCUS

To begin working toward a healthy view of men, and to understand their insecurities.

BEFORE YOU MEET

Before your group meets, read chapter 10 of *So Long, Insecurity*. As you read, highlight or underline parts that jump out to you. What rings true to you? What surprises you? What seems most challenging?

A WORD FROM BETH

{Note to the leader: You might want to read the following aloud to the group.}

I hope all of you were able to pray through chapter 9 last week. My prayer is that someday each of you will be able to look back and see this as a turning point in your life—the moment when you decided insecurity was no longer going to control you. May it be a fresh start for all of us new creatures in Christ as we find our security in Him.

This week we will talk about men—how we view them, the insecurities they deal with, and our unreasonable expectation that they will provide our security. Hear me on this: our discussion today is not just for married women or women involved in romantic relationships. Even if your last date was so long ago you can't see it in your rearview mirror, you have something to add to the conversation. All of us interact with men in various ways, whether they're our husbands or our boyfriends, or our fathers, sons, pastors, bosses, neighbors, or friends.

Women don't have a corner on the insecurity market. Men are insecure, too, even though they may show it in different ways. Let's have compassion on them as we have this discussion, remembering that they are, above all, our brothers in Christ.

DIGGING IN

As I share in chapter 10, a number of men responded to survey questions on my blog about their own insecurities. Choose a few of their responses to read aloud (see pages 181–187).

What areas do you notice as common sources of insecurity? Do any of these surprise you?

_____

_____

_____

wife's happiness, worries about infidelity, physical appearance, relationships, fear of failure

My son-in-law hit the nail on the head when he named fear of failure as men's number one insecurity.

> Two areas of potential failure floated to the top among the responses. In uncontested first place: failure to provide. The fear was so raw and so real that it stirred up significant compassion in me, shook loose a few preconceptions, and gave me a new appreciation for what men face. . . .
>
> The temptation [for men] to confuse who they are with what they make is astronomical. Add economic meltdowns, foreclosures, pay cuts, and layoffs to the landscape, and you've got yourself a serious breeding ground for insecurity. The thought occurred to me that the same culture that makes so many women feel inadequate physically makes just as many men feel inadequate financially. (pp. 186–187)

*Why do you think fear of failure tops the list of male insecurities? What pressures does our society place on men that feed these fears?

God created mankind in his own image, in the image of God he created them; male and female he created them. (Genesis 1:27)

*How might being aware of these fears give you insight into the men in your life (husband, father, son, brother, supervisor, etc.)?

_____

_____

_____

_____

_____

The survey also revealed that men tend to respond to insecurity differently than women.

> Overwhelmingly, the men used one word to describe what they do when they feel insecure: *withdraw*. If they don't overtly withdraw, they will probably behave in a way, whether consciously or unconsciously, that will make their loved ones withdraw. One way or the other, a man who feels insecure will often force space. . . . If quietness doesn't work, excessive irritation, agitation, or anger can usually do the job. . . . If we'd let it, the concept of withdrawal could explain so much to us. We think we're the only gender that gets eaten alive with insecurity because we don't recognize the opposite gender's signals. (pp. 194–195)

Have you observed this tendency to withdraw in the men in your life? How might interpreting this as a signal of insecurity change the way you react?

_____

_____

_____

_____

Why do I hammer the point that women don't have a monopoly on insecurity? Because too often we view men either as gods or as devils. We need to understand that they are as human as we are, with strengths and weaknesses, gifts and frailties. But too often we vacillate between adoring them and abhorring them, and neither extreme is healthy.

> On one hand, maybe we've elevated them so high in our thinking and given them so much credit for our soul's animation that we can't see their frailties. . . . [T]ake an honest appraisal of your preoccupation with men. Are you wholly unable to imagine being fulfilled without a man in pursuit or one in your clutches? We're particularly vulnerable to this brand of impaired vision if most of the affirmation we've received along the way has come from men. . . . If all your hopes are in men and all your dreams are spun around them like silver crowns on kings, you are not seeing clearly. . . . When our vision is blurred with distorted images, we can let the entire gender grow out of proportion in our romantic imaginations until we've begun to see them, you might say, as trees: towering, mighty, muscular trees. (pp. 197–198)

Give some examples from movies or books that illustrate our tendency as women to idealize men and see them as the solution to all our problems.

_____

_____

_____

_____

_____

*Can you think of any times in your life when you thought of men this way? How did it affect your relationships and sense of self-worth?

_____

_____

_____

_____

_____

On the other hand, our vision of men could be even more impaired by disdain. Maybe you've sustained considerable injury from them along the way. Life can set us up for some pretty devastating disappointments, especially those of us who were told in an unending stream of bedtime stories, books, and movies that someday our prince would come. For some of us, men were involved in our hardest blows and deepest heartbreaks. Or maybe it was just one man. Maybe then we shoved him up on a high hill as the icon of his entire gender and systematically sought out like individuals to confirm our suspicions. Once we compiled enough evidence to convict the lot, perhaps we bunched them all together until we could no longer see the forest for the trees. . . . Big, monstrous, ugly, gnarly trees. (pp. 198–199)

In what ways does our culture vilify men? As you consider movies, books, or current events, can you think of examples of this cynical, negative view of men?

_____

_____

_____

_____

How might having this attitude toward men affect the way we think about ourselves, our relationships, and perhaps even God?

_____

_____

_____

_____

_____

IN THE LIGHT OF THE WORD

In Mark 8:22-25 we read the account of Jesus restoring the blind man's sight (recounted in my book on page 195). This was a literal healing that must have amazed those who saw it and heard about it. And the same wonderful Jesus who touched this blind man's eyes can touch us, too, so we can see properly. It's no less miraculous when Jesus restores our spiritual vision, allowing us to see things (and people) clearly.

Let's look at some passages that give us clarity as we seek a correct perspective on men.

*Read Romans 3:21-24. What blunt truth does this passage tell us about humans, men and women alike? How does this truth keep us from either vilifying men or putting them on a pedestal?

_____

_____

_____

_____

_____

Read Genesis 1:26-27. What do men and women have in common, according to this passage? What does it mean to be made in God's image? What effect should this have on how we treat men or think about them?

_____

_____

_____

_____

_____

*Read Ephesians 4:1-6. According to this passage, how are we instructed to live with each other as believers? How might these qualities affect the way we interact with our Christian brothers?

_____

_____

_____

_____

_____

The only way we can develop a healthy, God-honoring view of humans—male or female—is to see them as God sees them. And the only way we learn to do that is from the Source Himself. When we keep our eyes on Him, incredible things can happen. Our whole way of thinking can be realigned.

*Read Matthew 14:22-32. What fears and barriers was Peter able to overcome when he kept his eyes on Christ? Why was he able to do this?

_____

_____

_____

_____

_____

fear of the storm, fear that Jesus was a ghost, fear of the impossible (knowing he shouldn't be able to walk on water!)

*What happened when Peter noticed the wind and looked down at the waves?

_____

_____

_____

_____

_____

All have sinned and fall short of the glory of God, and all are justified freely by his grace through the redemption that came by Christ Jesus. (Romans 3:23-24)

We sometimes criticize Peter for losing his nerve so quickly, but let's not forget the guts it took to step out of the boat in the first place. Peter was a fisherman and had spent a lot of time on the water. He knew very well that according to all the normal, natural laws, it was physically impossible for him to step onto that water. Yet when his eyes and thoughts were fixed on Jesus, he was able to get out of the boat. He knew that if Jesus was calling him, nothing else mattered. The storm was scary, but Jesus was more powerful. The water was wild and wet and decidedly not solid ground, but Jesus could transform it. Peter knew that on his own he was weak and sinful and afraid, but with Jesus in front of him, all of that faded away.

*Can you relate to Peter? Share a time when focusing on Christ enabled you to overcome fears or barriers.

_____

_____

_____

_____

_____

When we keep our eyes on Jesus, everything else—even the scary stuff, even our biggest hang-ups about men, even our elephant-sized insecurities—will fade. Looking at Christ helps us regain our perspective.

*Let's finish by reading Hebrews 12:1-2. Where should we fix our eyes? How does that perspective change the way we view others around us?

_____

_____

_____

_____

_____

WRAP-UP

Conclude this week's discussion by reading this quote from pages 200–201:

> Oh, that we would not fight the touch of that healing hand on our chins, urging us to lift our faces to the sky. We are bereft of clear vision toward man—or woman—until we look up steadfastly at our wise and one and only Savior. . . .

When you've stared at the face of Christ long enough through the lens of Scripture, you will begin to look around you and see men clearly. No longer like trees, walking. No longer like gods or devils. Just fellow sojourners with God-given dignity—and feet of clay.

As time permits, ask women to share their needs, and take time to pray for each other.

ON YOUR OWN

- In a journal, consider the flawed ways you have viewed men. You may want to think about a few specific men who have played significant roles in your life and evaluate your attitude toward them. Have you erred toward adoring them or abhorring them? Confess this to God and ask Him to correct your perspective.
- Write out Hebrews 12:1-2 and put it somewhere you will see it often. Each time you read it this week, ask God to help you fix your eyes on Jesus.

Letting God Be God

I am certain that God, who began the good work within you, will continue his work until it is finally finished on the day when Christ Jesus returns.

Philippians 1:6, NLT

WARM-UP

Go around the room and have each woman choose one of the following questions to answer briefly:

What would be your dream job?

What music have you been listening to lately?

Share a birthday memory from your childhood. What made that birthday special?

After everyone has had a chance to share, open your discussion time with this question:

Last week we talked about focusing on Christ and letting Him transform the way we see other people. How has this idea influenced your thinking this week?

_____

_____

_____

_____

_____

THIS WEEK'S FOCUS

To recognize and let go of our tendency to play God or play the devil with men.

BEFORE YOU MEET

Before your group meets, read chapters 11 and 12 of *So Long, Insecurity.* As you read, highlight or underline parts that jump out to you. What rings true to you? What surprises you? What seems most challenging?

A WORD FROM BETH

{Note to the leader: You might want to read the following aloud to the group.}

I have a feeling some of you might not be thrilled to be here today. There are some tough things we have to face about our own tendencies as women that frankly don't make us look so good. It can be difficult to face head-on the ways our insecurity can damage relationships and hurt the people closest to us—husband, children, other family members, close friends. I won't pretend this process is pleasant, but there's no other way than to hold up the mirror and face reality. It's time for us to be honest about how our fears sometimes hijack the best relationships we have going for us—and then figure out how to change that.

We're coming down the homestretch of this study, and the most encouraging, practical material is still ahead. I encourage you to press on. In the spirit of 2 Corinthians 8:11, "Now finish the work, so that your eager willingness to do it may be matched by your completion of it." Translation? Let's finish strong!

DIGGING IN

Let's start by touching on some of the survey results I share in chapter 12. Based on the way the men responded to questions about how women exhibit insecurity, it's clear that we're not hiding our issues nearly as well as we think we are. Men see what we're doing, and by and large, they're not impressed.

What were some of the things men pointed out in women as signs of insecurity? Does this list seem accurate to you? What surprises you about the survey respondents' perceptions?

_____

_____

_____

_____

_____

incessant talking, dressing provocatively, promiscuity, unrealistic relationship expectations, irrational jealousies, emotional episodes, obsession with what others think, insatiable need for affirmation

Some of the men expressed frustration about constantly having to reassure the women in their life. One husband wrote about his frustrations:

> Typical, common, widespread insecurities include looks, body shapes, lack of education or perceived intelligence, neediness, and many others. It manifests itself in nagging, self-doubt, self-loathing, seeking approval/validation, and the need for constant reassurance. It gets quite tiring for men who, as we get older, just love *you* for exactly the way you are. Can you not understand that? We are not lying if we tell you we love you, you are beautiful and appealing, and we enjoy being with you immensely. When women's insecurities are vividly displayed to us, it turns us off, frustrates us to no extent, and perplexes us. Get over it! (pp. 236–237)

*How do you react to this statement? In what ways has insecurity affected your relationships with the men around you?

_____

_____

_____

_____

_____

Men *are* repelled by open displays of female insecurity. In the long run, it does not make them more tender to us, more careful with us, more loving toward us, or more attached to us. It makes them, in the words of another guy, want to "run for [their] lives." It may not be fair, but it is a fact.

After months of research, I'm convinced that men are indeed more intrigued by a confident woman who carries herself well and knows who she is than a picture-perfect beauty who seems little more than that. Some men might be tempted to take the latter to bed, but when all is said and done, they would more likely take the former to *heart*. When the average guy sees the woman in his life hold her own in the face of intimidation, he is impressed. At the end of the day, both men and women want to be with someone they can respect. (p. 237)

*How might your relationship with your husband (or a man you're interested in) change if you were characterized by security and confidence? Does the prospect of healthier relationships provide you with additional motivation to deal with your insecurity?

_____

_____

_____

_____

_____

In chapter 11 we take a long, hard look at our own gender and begin with a truth we might prefer to ignore: sometimes as women we play the devil with men. Fueled by our insecurities, we get a heady feeling of power when we sense we can use our femininity to shake a man.

There's something about a man of conviction—whether he belongs to us or not—that makes the most dangerous kind of unhealthy women want to break him. It's a sad admission that sometimes women simply aren't satisfied unless they think a man would choose them over God. (p. 205)

Can you think of an example from real life when a woman tried to change a man's convictions? What do you think motivated her?

_____

_____

_____

_____

_____

LORD my God, you
are very great; you
are clothed with
splendor and majesty.
(Psalm 104:1)

Keep in mind that the convictions we're talking about don't just have to be sexual. The sad truth is that sometimes we feel threatened if our man is truly on fire for the Lord because somehow we think his passion for God negates his passion for us. If that sense of threat causes us to do whatever we can to break down his enthusiasm and drag him back to a safe middle ground, we're in big trouble. When we deliberately pull a man down from his God-given convictions, we are playing the devil—and we need to recognize it and stop.

*If you feel comfortable sharing, when have you felt threatened by the convictions of a man in your life? What do you think was behind your fear?

_____

_____

_____

_____

_____

Most of us realize at some level that tempting men to abandon their convictions is wrong. But the other extreme—trying to play God to our men—can be even more dangerous because of its subtlety. Let's look at two divine attributes many insecure women want to pursue: omnipotence and omniscience.

Although humans can't attain total power, knowing that fact hasn't kept us from trying. The most we can successfully achieve is excessive control. . . . People who are chronically insecure often have an overwhelming tendency to become control freaks. Upon serious consideration, that inclination makes perfect sense. We feel most secure when our environment is in control, and since no one is able to control it to our satisfaction, we decide we have to do it ourselves. If someone would do it and do it right, we wouldn't have to take over, so it's not really our fault, we reason. It's our responsibility. . . .

An insecure person's greatest need for control is directed toward those who have the most potential to either threaten her security *or* strengthen it. That is why women choose boyfriends or husbands as the primary candidates for control. These men have the greatest capacity to affect our sense of personal well-being and security, and they pose the biggest threat. Children also have the power to rock a woman's world, so the more insecure a mother is, the more she fights to control her children. (pp. 208–209)

*Whom do you find yourself most wanting to control? What do you think is the connection between insecurity and a desire for control?

_____

_____

_____

_____

_____

How is appropriate parental authority different from excessive parental control?

_____

_____

_____

_____

_____

The tough part about our battle with being controlling is that often our goal is honorable. Our hearts are actually in the right place!

> I believe our greatest challenge as women is to avoid trying to control someone toward what we're genuinely convinced is a better life. The more insecure we are, the more tempting it is because something is in it for us, too. In other words, if my loved one would _____ , then I'd be _____ . (p. 210)

How would you fill in the blanks above?

_____

_____

_____

_____

_____

*What are some ways we can combat the tendency to play God in the lives of those we love?

_____

_____

_____

_____

_____

Here's the bottom line about control:

> It took me forty years in the wilderness to realize that at the end of the day, people do what they want to do. You can't make them do something else. You can't force them. You can't change them. You can't deliver them. Only God can. And that's why He's omnipotent and we're not.
>
> We are not in charge. Somewhere along the way, we each have to acknowledge that our loved one is a separate person from us—someone God loves, pursues, and when necessary, chastises. When we try to do God's job, we get in God's way. We are called to cherish, support, and pray for others, but tying our security to them is a lost cause. That knot we keep tightening is no more fair to them than it is to us. Hand that rope over to God. Let Him undo that tangled-up mess and retie your security to Himself. He's the One with all the power. (p. 214)

*Have you ever come up against the realization that you can't change anyone? What were the circumstances?

_____

_____

_____

_____

_____

Let's move on now to the second way we too often try to be like God: omniscience, or the desire to know it all. In our insecurity we want to know everything, because how can we control what we don't know? But trying to know more than what's healthy for us can cause deep wounds. On pages 215–218 I tell the story of a young woman whose desire to know more and more details about her former fiancé's indiscretions led her into a situation she could barely escape. When she shared her story with me, I told her, "You've eaten from the tree of the knowledge of good and evil. You wanted to know what God knew."

I'm not a proponent of ignorance or denial. The pursuit of knowledge for the edification of soul and community is a priority passion. But that kind of positive result comes from eating from the "tree of life," metaphorically speaking, not from "the tree of the knowledge of good and evil" (Genesis 2:9, 17). . . .

I believe those two trees in humanity's first garden were living symbols of these very concepts. One promoted life. The other promoted death. Because God is complete perfection and immutable holiness, He can handle omniscience. He can know all things—good and evil—without responding with sin, weakness, horror, or despair. We, on the other hand, don't have that luxury. Think how many times we've begged someone to tell us something and sworn we could handle it only to flip like a flapjack the second it was out of the person's mouth.

What God initiates, He equips us to handle. . . .

When we scratch and claw to dig information out of the dirt, however, we don't get the same kind of grace that accompanies divine revelation. God graciously forgives, restores, and even resurrects as we bring Him our needs, but the pursuit of omniscience costs us dearly in the meantime. (pp. 218–219)

Have you ever found yourself in a situation where you asked for more information than you could handle? What happened?

_____

_____

_____

_____

_____

*Have you ever sensed that God was setting limits on your knowledge based on what you can handle? Have you ever set boundaries for what you should or should not know? How do you know when you're crossing a boundary?

_____

_____

_____

_____

_____

IN THE LIGHT OF THE WORD

As we jump into the Scripture passages today, we'll look at some of the ways we try to play God. I want to help us regain a right perspective on God. Because, as we talked about last week, when we see Him clearly, everything else falls into place. Let's face it: there's only one being in this universe who has omnipotence and omniscience, and He's not us.

My hope is that when we get even a glimpse of His power and knowledge, we'll realize that He really doesn't need any help. We'll let Him be God and let ourselves be human.

*Read Psalm 104:24-32. As someone reads out loud, think about the wonderful images of God's power that are included.

_____

_____

_____

_____

_____

What phrases or images stand out most to you? How is God's power—his omnipotence—communicated?

_____

_____

_____

_____

_____

*Read Isaiah 55:8-11. What does it mean that the Lord's thoughts are higher than ours?

_____

_____

_____

_____

_____

How does a bigger, more accurate picture of God help us gain perspective on ourselves and our limitations?

_____

_____

_____

_____

God alone is omnipotent. He alone is omniscient. He alone has the power to transform hearts. And He will always accomplish His purposes!

Read 1 Thessalonians 5:23-24. How is God changing us? What does He promise in this passage?

_____
_____
_____
_____
_____

"My thoughts are not your thoughts, neither are your ways my ways," declares the LORD. (Isaiah 55:8)

*Read Philippians 1:3-6. What is Paul confident about (verse 6)? How can this assurance give us hope—and cure us of our desire to change others?

_____
_____
_____
_____
_____

WRAP-UP

Reading these passages that describe our almighty God should stop us in our tracks and humble us. Who are we fooling when we try to be like God? Let Him be in control of everything; we can't do it anyway. Let Him know all things; we'll be content with only what is right for us to know. Let Him be in the business of changing us and those around us. In other words . . . let God be God.

As time permits, ask women to share their needs, and take time to pray for each other.

- If you have experienced a situation where you grasped for more information than you could handle, ask the Lord for His help and healing this week. Pray for the ability to discern and respect the boundaries He sets for you.

- Think about the situations in your life that tempt you to try to be omnipotent or omniscient. What do you need to let go of? Ask God to help you develop a plan for dealing with these temptations.

- If you're feeling brave, consider asking your spouse or a close friend how you and/or your relationship could benefit from your increased security. What steps can you take this week in that direction?

The Power to Choose

*Do not throw away your confidence; it will be richly
    rewarded. You need to persevere so that when you have
    done the will of God, you will receive what he has
    promised.*

HEBREWS 10:35-36

WARM-UP

*Go around the room and have each woman choose one of the
following questions to answer briefly:*
    What is your favorite season?
    Share a good memory you have of one of your grandparents.
    *What kind of service or volunteer work do you gravitate
toward? How do you enjoy helping others?*

*After everyone has had a chance to share, open your discussion
time with this question:*

***What legacy of faith and womanhood have you received
from the women who have gone before you?**

_____

_____

_____

_____

_____

THIS WEEK'S FOCUS

To realize we have the
power, with God's help,
to choose our reactions,
and to think about how
our choices affect the
legacy we are leaving
the women who come
behind us.

BEFORE YOU MEET

Before your group
meets, read chapters 13
and 14 of *So Long,
Insecurity.* As you read,
highlight or underline
parts that jump out to
you. What rings true
to you? What surprises
you? What seems most
challenging?

A WORD FROM BETH

{Note to the leader: You might want to read the following aloud to the group.}

I'm excited for this week's discussion. We've spent some valuable time laying the groundwork to help us understand why we struggle with insecurity and what triggers it. We've looked at errors in our thinking—about ourselves and about men—and we've started to correct those. We've talked about looking at Jesus to regain perspective, and about letting go of our desire to play God. This week we get to move into more practical, hands-on material: what do we do when our insecurity is triggered?

Maybe for years you've been reacting the same way. You feel threatened, your insecurity raises its ugly head, and almost before you can blink, you've melted into a puddle of hysterical neediness. Trust me, I've been there—and it's not pretty. But hear me on this: it doesn't have to be that way. No matter how entrenched a pattern is in our lives, we are not doomed to be stuck in it forever. Our God is a God of transformation! He is in the business of changing lives. But He will not do it without our consent. We have to be willing to enter into the process. And once we begin, we can use one of the potent tools God has given us: the power to choose.

DIGGING IN

Let's recap a few points from chapter 13:

> The most prized possession God gave humankind when He formed Adam from the dust of the earth was the power to choose. Nowhere do we bear the image of our Creator more forthrightly than in the ability to exercise our free will. . . .
>
> By choosing to have a different reaction *even prior to having a different emotion*, we can effect an immediate sense of heightened security. The reaction leads to a new feeling, and the new feeling leads to more consistent reactions. The result? We spiral up.

One of the most common human claims is that we can't change the way we feel. That may be true, but we *can* change the way we think, which will change the way we act. And as we change the way we act, the way we feel also begins to change. In the breaking of every habit, someone wills it first and feels it later. (pp. 239–241)

How do you respond to this idea that our feelings follow our thoughts and actions? Does it seem possible? Does it give you hope?

_____

_____

_____

_____

_____

*Have your emotions ever changed in response to your actions? Describe a time when you chose to act a certain way because it was the right thing to do, even though it was contrary to your emotions at the time. What happened?

_____

_____

_____

_____

_____

We can begin by changing our actions in response to a trigger, perhaps by doing something as simple as imagining how a secure person would respond and then imitating it. That action brings our security—born of our identity in Christ— to the surface. That can get us through one incident. But to see broader, lasting transformation, we also need to change our attitude. Here's the reality:

We will always have triggers of insecurity, but *we* get to decide whether or not we're going to take the bait. I don't recommend having no reaction. We are human beings with God-given emotions and visceral responses that don't always show up politely. One reason God wrapped our souls in limber flesh was to give our emotions a means of expression. I recommend that you refuse insecurity the right to stalk every other reaction. If you're like me, these may be refreshing new revelations for you:

We can be hurt without also being insecure.

We can be disappointed without also being insecure.

We can be shocked without also being insecure.

We can be unsure without also being insecure.

We can even be humbled without also being insecure.

(pp. 243–244)

In other words, we set boundaries on insecurity. We acknowledge the hurt, but we don't allow it to touch the deeper part of us—our sense of worth and value. We don't allow it to cause us to question our key relationships. We don't allow it to erode our identity as God's beloved children.

Are there certain emotions that seem to trigger insecurity for you? How can we keep insecurity from tagging along with other emotions?

_____

_____

_____

_____

_____

Being secure doesn't mean always being on an even keel. God made us to experience emotions, and in fact, He also experiences emotions! But our feelings don't have to be paired with insecurity, and they don't have to drive the way we respond to situations.

*On pages 244–245 I give several examples of "self-talk": deliberate statements you can say to yourself when your insecurities are triggered. Have you ever tried this? What was the result? Which of these statements seem most helpful to you?

He put a new song in my mouth, a hymn of praise to our God. Many will see and fear the LORD and put their trust in him. (Psalm 40:3)

_____

_____

_____

_____

_____

On page 246 I write the following:

> God gave you your security, and nobody gets to force it from you. You must make up your mind that the only way someone can take it from you is for you to hand it over. You have the right to hold on to security for dear life in every situation and every relationship. It's the power of choice.

*Does it surprise you to think that you have the power to choose security? How would your life be different if you held on to security "for dear life"?

_____

_____

_____

_____

_____

*What practical steps can you take to help change the way you think? (Some of my suggestions are on page 257.)

_____

_____

_____

_____

I spend a lot of time in chapter 13 dealing with unhealthy relationships, emotional predators, and what I'll call emotional wrecks. We'll just touch on that here, but let me reiterate that if you find yourself struggling to make good choices in a relationship you know is unhealthy or dangerous, please seek counsel and assistance.

I use the devastating problem of pornography as an example of how women can deal with difficult issues, even in our closest relationships, without giving way to insecurity. It's far too easy for us to convince ourselves that someone else's problem is all about us. We own it, and then, as a result, we watch every drop of our security drain away. That is a recipe for disaster.

It's imperative, for our own good and our mate's, that we learn to confront an offense and set a boundary. As I write on page 255, "_Agape_ is a kind of love that is in another person's best interest. To stand back and watch a spouse spin further and further out of control without ever attempting to confront, set a boundary, or permit consequences is not in his (or your) best interest."

In what areas do you tend to let others' problems erode your security? How can you combat this? What boundaries might you need to set?

_____

_____

_____

_____

_____

Choosing to change the way we think and react takes effort. We have to retrain ourselves to stop in that first moment of a trigger and call to mind the unalterable truth that we are clothed with strength and dignity! When we have our minds in the right place, our actions—and later our emotions—will follow. It's almost like an aggressive two-year-old (I've known one or two) who has to be reminded over and over that hitting is not an acceptable response when a friend takes his or her toy. It takes time. It takes patience. It takes teaching what to do, not just what not to do. But eventually the new response comes. (How many twenty-year-olds do you know who swat their friends in frustration?)

And here we reach a key point of chapter 14: even if we think the effort needed to change is too much, even if for our own sakes we would just muddle through the rest of our lives entrenched in our old patterns, the story changes when we consider how our choices affect others. When we think about the legacy we're passing on to our children, grandchildren, or other people in our lives, we may suddenly find we're willing to make the change.

Can you think of things worth doing for someone else that you might not do for yourself?

_____

_____

_____

_____

_____

The answer to this question could be as mundane as taking prenatal vitamins or exercising to have energy to play with the grandkids. Or it could be as complicated as dealing with addiction or changing unhealthy communication habits. Encourage group members to share at a level they're comfortable with.

Here's something to think about from the end of chapter 14:

> Just because we have estrogen milking up our bloodstream doesn't mean we have to carry on the insecurities of a preteen girl. We really can grow up. As hard as it is, we really can take responsibility. We really can find freedom. We can sit around and think about how pathetic we are, or we really can pursue some healing—for ourselves and for that preteen girl. You and I . . . have got to make a definitive decision to be strong for our daughters. And don't even try handing me the excuse that you're not a mom so this doesn't apply to you. The entire generation of adult women in any culture is systematically raising the next, whether they mean to be or not. Every acne-faced middle school girl you pass in the mall, texting on her cell phone or checking out that older guy in the food court, is your daughter. What are you going to do about her? What would you be willing to do *for* her? (p. 273)

*What legacy do you want to pass on to the next generation of women?

_____

_____

_____

_____

_____

IN THE LIGHT OF THE WORD

In these chapters I've challenged you—and myself—to take a big step. We *can* exercise that power to choose, and we *can* make a change. In this section we'll look at some Scriptures that remind us that God is on our side in this battle. He has given us the power to choose, and He will help us exercise it. He is the one who does the changing, but we have to be willing to take each next step.

One of the first things we can change is our thinking. If you've ever read through the Psalms, you know that David and the other psalmists provide plenty of evidence of their humanness. They're not on some superspiritual plane, far above the world's problems. When we read some of their words, we sense anger, doubt, fear, and grief. But they also call themselves back to the right perspective—often by praising the Lord.

*Read Psalm 42. What complaints does the writer of this psalm make? What emotions does he express?

_____

_____

_____

_____

_____

The same words are used as a refrain in verses 5 and 11. What does the psalmist remind himself of here? What can we learn from this passage about changing our attitudes by first changing our thinking?

_____

_____

_____

_____

_____

Read Deuteronomy 30:19-20, taking note of the power we are given to choose. What are the Israelites being encouraged to choose in this passage? What benefits are promised as a result of that choice?

_____

_____

_____

_____

_____

The Israelites were about to go into the Promised Land after forty years of wandering in the desert—forty years that passed because of the previous generation's lack of faith in the very God who had rescued them from Egypt. Now, much like us, they were presented with a choice. If they followed the Lord, He would be life to them! If they chased after idols, they would be moving away from the Lord's blessing.

The Lord is setting before us abundant life—full of love and purpose and security. The choice is ours!

What do you think it means to choose life? Can you think of some specific examples?

_____

_____

_____

_____

_____

Why, my soul, are you downcast? Why so disturbed within me? Put your hope in God, for I will yet praise him, my Savior and my God. (Psalm 42:11)

The Israelites didn't just have to make a choice once and for all. The next several books of the Old Testament illustrate that they had to choose time and again. Just like us, they made right choices followed by wrong ones. They forgot about the Lord's blessings and had to remind themselves over and over.

It's easy to get discouraged when we repeat our mistakes. But we don't give up! We know that the Holy Spirit is working in our hearts. We are called to persevere.

*Read Philippians 3:7-14. What is Paul trying to gain? Based on this passage, what things does he value?

_____

_____

_____

_____

_____

How might these verses encourage us as we seek transformation?

_____

_____

_____

_____

_____

93

The apostle Paul is both the ultimate idealist and the ultimate realist. He sees so clearly the fundamental goal of all who believe in Christ: to be found in Christ, to know Him, to become like Him. In other words, to be transformed! But Paul is honest enough to note that he's not there yet. He doesn't dwell on what is past, but he strains with all his energy to move forward. May we share his passion and his forward vision as we seek to leave a strong legacy for those behind us.

WRAP-UP

When we allow the Lord to heal us and change us, we can have a powerful testimony to others. As I write in chapter 14,

> God cured me of my own gross unfaithfulness. He healed my unloveliness with His own love. As I live and breathe, I am not the woman I used to be, but the fact is, I started this journey because I wasn't yet the woman that I wanted to be. . . .
>
> As long as we're here in these human bodies on the topsoil of planet Earth instead of six feet under shoving up weeds, we'll always have a few places that could use some curing. And we won't need curing just for our own sakes. (pp. 270–271)

Psalm 40:1-3 says, "I waited patiently for the LORD; he turned to me and heard my cry. He lifted me out of the slimy pit, out of the mud and mire; he set my feet on a rock and gave me a firm place to stand. He put a new song in my mouth, a hymn of praise to our God. Many will see and fear the LORD and put their trust in him." May others put their trust in the Lord when they see His work in our lives.

As time permits, ask women to share their needs, and take time to pray for each other.

ON YOUR OWN

- Write out scripts that will help you combat the most common insecurity triggers you face. (See pages 244–245 for some ideas.)

- Ask the Lord for insight as you consider whether there is anything in your close relationships that you need to confront or change. What boundaries might you need to set?

- In a journal, write out in detail what legacy you want to leave to the women who come behind you. How do you want them to view themselves? What do you need to deal with so you can set a strong example? Ask the Lord to reveal areas where you need His transforming power in your life.

Looking beyond Ourselves

Your light will break forth like the dawn, and your healing
will quickly appear; then your righteousness will go before
you, and the glory of the LORD will be your rear guard.
Then you will call, and the LORD will answer; you will
cry for help, and he will say: Here am I.

ISAIAH 58:8-9

WARM-UP

Go around the room and have each woman choose one of the
following questions to answer briefly:

    What is one thing you look forward to doing every summer?
    Share a good memory from a childhood family vacation.
    What is one of your favorite restaurants?

After everyone has had a chance to share, open your discussion
time with this question:

What do your closest female friendships mean to you?
How do you deal with hurt or insecurity in the context
of these friendships?

THIS WEEK'S FOCUS

To consider practical ways we can help each other in our battle with insecurity, and to learn to look beyond our fears to find our greater purpose in life.

BEFORE YOU MEET

Before your group meets, read chapters 15 and 16 of *So Long, Insecurity*. As you read, highlight or underline parts that jump out to you. What rings true to you? What surprises you? What seems most challenging?

A WORD FROM BETH

{Note to the leader: You might want to read the following aloud to the group.}

In this week's discussion we can start moving the focus off our own insecurity. We will be thinking not just about how we experience triggers to insecurity but about other women and how we can help them deal with their triggers.

I'll admit that when I invite women to share their vulnerabilities with each other, I'm suggesting something a little scary. Because let's be honest: a struggling junior high girl who tells the popular girls that they make her feel insecure is, unfortunately, just asking for more of the same. But we're not in junior high anymore, sisters (and praise the Lord for that!). In some ways, we're all both the struggling girl and the popular girl. We all wrestle with insecurities, and we all (knowingly or not) do things that make others feel insecure. So let's be open with each other and respond to that openness with support, respect, and honesty.

DIGGING IN

When I surveyed men about their take on women's insecurities, one respondent said this:

> Most obvious is when women are around other women; they try to size each other up and look for reasons to not get along rather than to get along. They seem easily intimidated, whether by physical beauty, character status, or whatever makes them feel that the other woman has more going for her, and a barrier goes up. (pp. 275–276)

How do you respond to this take on female relationships? Has insecurity ever robbed you of what could have been a rich friendship with another woman? Has it affected the type of woman you befriend?

_____

_____

_____

_____

_____

I have to admit that there's more than a snippet of truth to what this man says. We women do sometimes let barriers come between us—and that's a terrible shame. Let's do our best to break this mold by taking a look at four things we can do to promote security among the women around us. First, we need to *stop making comparisons*.

> Our constant propensity to compare ourselves to the women around us is wrecking our perceptions of both ourselves and them. Most of us aren't in a public place for five minutes before we peruse the female players in the room and judge where we rank. . . .
>
> But we can stop playing the game even if no one else in our environment signs the no-compete. If we don't think we can, we're not giving ourselves enough credit. When we work from an activated mentality of God-given security, we are fully capable of thinking another woman is beautiful without concluding we are ugly. We can esteem another woman's achievements without feeling like an idiot. We can admire another woman's terrific shape without feeling like a slob. Where on earth did we come up with the idea that we have to subtract value from ourselves in order to give credit to someone else? (pp. 279–280)

*Talk about a time you fell victim to the "bad math" of insecurity (see pages 280–281). How can we correct our thinking when this happens?

_____

_____

_____

_____

_____

Second, we need to start personalizing the other woman.

> In order to nurse a rival mentality, we almost always view our competitor through a one-dimensional lens. She is not a person. She is a contender. If she got the guy we wanted, we don't see her in terms of a multilayered life of ups and downs, self-doubts, and second guesses. We depersonalize her into a manipulator or a relationship wrecker. It's easier to despise her that way. . . .
>
> I . . . think that if we view potential contenders as equally broken people with real problems, pain, hopes, dreams, and disappointments, we will have taken the first step toward unraveling a rivalry. No one lives on this planet long without scars. The woman who hurt you— whoever she may be and whatever the circumstance—has also been hurt. Either we can keep stabbing each other back or we can lay down the sword.
>
> In Jesus' name. (pp. 284, 286)

*Have you ever felt your insecure or jealous feelings evaporate when something occurred that humanized your "rival"? What happened?

_____

_____

_____

Third, we don't trip another woman's insecurity switch.

We all have just enough meanness in us to occasionally enjoy a peck or two at somebody we know to be weak. Maybe we're usually compassionate, but every now and then we're in a mischievous or terse mood or maybe just tired of tiptoeing around a person who needs to deal with her issues. No matter what's driving us to pick at somebody, let's keep in mind that only insecure people enjoy tripping another person's insecurity switch. Every time we're tempted to do it, we're probably having an attack of our own and trying to build up our wounded selves at somebody else's expense. (pp. 288–289)

*Telling someone else that you're feeling insecure requires great vulnerability. How would you react if someone came to you with a situation like those described on pages 287–288 and humbly suggested that you were acting as a trigger? How could good friends or family members handle this?

We will not compare ourselves with each other as if one of us were better and another worse. We have far more interesting things to do with our lives. Each of us is an original. (Galatians 5:26, *The Message*)

Mind you, some women are so insecure, there's not enough you can do, wear, or say to shield them, and to be honest, they're the ones who need to get the big grip. Try this for the balance when you can't decide if your sensitivity is helping them or hurting them: the goal in our female relationships should be to encourage one another's security. Not enable one another's *in*security.

If we simply help each other stay chronically insecure, we've accomplished nothing. I want my closest female associates to offer me a relatively safe place to grow in my security, not wear themselves out over my lack of it. (p. 289)

How can we find the balance between not tripping another woman's insecurity switch and not taking responsibility for another woman's feelings?

_____

_____

_____

_____

_____

The fourth way we help others is to *be examples of secure women.*

Most women will . . . never believe that a secure woman is a real, live possibility until they see one face-to-face. Problem-to-problem. Threat-to-threat. Chase-to-grace. If you'll become the first example in your sphere of influence, you won't be the last. You may pop up all by your lonely self in the beginning, but soon another will pop up close by, then another, because it's as contagious as its counterpart. (p. 290)

*Who have been examples of secure women in your life? What impact have they had on you?

_____

_____

_____

_____

_____

Remember the story of my friend Stacy (see pages 291–292)? While getting ready for a prestigious event, she stopped herself in the middle of an insecure frenzy and said to herself, "But I have this Treasure!" The reference is from 2 Corinthians 4:6-7: "God, who said, 'Let light shine out of darkness,' made his light shine in our hearts to give us the light of the knowledge of God's glory displayed in the face of Christ. But we have this treasure in jars of clay to show that this all-surpassing power is from God and not from us."

> Did you hear that? We have this treasure! We are aflame with God's glory and radiating with the light of His knowledge in the exquisite face of His Son, Jesus Christ. And we're *insecure*? What kind of lies have we believed all this time? We, of all people on the earth, possess the reason, the residence, and the ongoing revelation to be, of all things, most secure.
>
> By the time my friend was finished testifying, I was nearly on my feet, and my heart was a flood of fresh faith. That's the way women are meant to build one another up in God-given security. (p. 293)

What kind of testimony would you like to have to share with others? How can we encourage other women to find their God-given security?

_____

_____

_____

_____

_____

When we cultivate this kind of focus—taking our minds off ourselves and thinking of others first—our whole perspective changes. Our culture tells us to major on the minors, to embrace the superficial, to spend our time and energy worrying about ourselves. And guess what? That's a prime recipe for insecurity. We have to find the way out. Here's how I put it in chapter 16:

> Human nature dictates that most often we will be as insecure as we are self-absorbed. The best possible way to keep from getting sucked into the superficial, narcissistic mentality that money, possessions, and sensuality can satisfy and secure us is to deliberately give ourselves to something much greater. We are under the constant indoctrination that getting is the way to receiving.
>
> Christ, the Author of life more abundant, taught something totally different. He showed us that giving, rather than getting, is the means to receiving. I will say it again before our journey ends: to find yourself, your true, secure self, you must lose yourself in something larger. (pp. 309–310)

*Tell about a time when serving God or focusing on someone else freed you from the self-absorption of insecurity. Why do you think this happens?

_____

_____

_____

_____

_____

For many of us, God used painful experiences to birth our life passions. A fire burns in me to see women of all ages and colors freed and flourishing in Christ, because I've known the anguish of bondage and abuse. I have a friend who was profoundly affected by abandonment and now pours her life into helping couples adopt. I know of another woman who struggled in school and didn't get her GED until well into adulthood. She now helps children learn how to read. . . .

You are meant to be a miracle too. Your past has not come full circle to its complete redemption until you allow Christ to not only defuse it, but also to use it. I'm not suggesting that you have to go public with all your sins and sorrows. I'm simply proposing that the only reason God allowed all that pain in your path, as much as He loved you, was to bring good from it. Have you offered Him the freedom to work all those hardships together for good as He promises in His Word to those who love Him and seek to fulfill His purposes? [See Romans 8:28.] (pp. 310–311)

Have you ever known someone whose passion was connected to her deepest point of pain? How can God redeem the darkest things of our lives for His glory?

_____

_____

_____

_____

_____

Someone once told me that in the midst of her struggles she prayed, "God, don't let this pain be wasted." There's no escaping the sorrows, the fears, the tragedies, the insecurities that face us in this life. But when we allow our sovereign Lord to redeem our pain—to use it for His purposes—it is not wasted. It becomes a means of refining and a path to grace.

IN THE LIGHT OF THE WORD

Let's begin this section by talking about the wonderful passage from Isaiah 58 that I quote in chapter 16 (pp. 317–318). Before you read the verses, keep in mind the context. The Israelites were asking why God seemed not to hear them when they prayed. They held up their fasting as proof of their righteousness, but the Lord indicted them with their own actions. They patted themselves on the back because they went to the Temple, but otherwise they did as they pleased (verse 3). They were oppressing their own workers, and even their days of fasting were ruined by quarrels and violence. They pretended to do the right things, but in reality, they were self-absorbed and superficial—and probably miserable as a result.

*Read Isaiah 58:6-11. What do verses 6-7 tell us about the attitude God wants us to have toward others?

_____

_____

_____

_____

_____

*According to verses 8-11, what will happen when we adjust our attitude outward instead of inward? What images are used to communicate the idea of renewal and refreshment?

_____

_____

_____

_____

_____

There's no question that the world benefits when we break free of our self-absorption and serve others. But the amazing thing is that _we_ benefit as well. When we have a sense of purpose that goes beyond our own skin, we are renewed, refreshed, and satisfied.

As we think about moving our focus beyond ourselves, let's look at some Scripture passages that address our relationships with other women. Keep your eyes open to ways we can build each other up and help each other find security.

Read Galatians 5:22-26. How does celebrating each person's uniqueness help us avoid jealousy and unhealthy comparisons? What role does the Holy Spirit play in helping us accomplish this?

_____

_____

_____

_____

_____

The Holy Spirit produces this kind of fruit in our lives: love, joy, peace, patience, kindness, goodness, faithfulness, gentleness, and self-control. There is no law against these things! (Galatians 5:22-23, NLT)

I love the way The Message *paraphrases Galatians 5:26: "We will not compare ourselves with each other as if one of us were better and another worse. We have far more interesting things to do with our lives. Each of us is an original."*

*Read John 13:34-35. What is Jesus' command here? What are some specific things that would happen if we followed it?

_____

_____

_____

_____

_____

*When we get caught up in insecurity, too often we depersonalize those who threaten us. How does loving someone keep us from viewing her only as a competitor?

_____

_____

_____

_____

_____

Read Matthew 5:43-45. Why do you think we are commanded to pray for our enemies? How does the act of praying for them—or for people who just rub us the wrong way, threaten us, and trigger every possible insecurity button—change us?

_____

_____

_____

_____

_____

WRAP-UP

We'll never be healed of our self-centeredness until we are wounded irreparably with love for an aching world. Insecurity puts us in a prison of self-absorption, but when we reach out to others, those prison bars are shattered. Sharing the love of Christ will become life to us, bringing us renewal, perspective, and purpose. May we leave our superficiality behind and reap the benefits God will graciously bestow.

As time permits, ask women to share their needs, and take time to pray for each other.

ON YOUR OWN

- Think through your closest female relationships. What things do others do that trip your insecurity switch? Are there things you're doing that likely trip other people's triggers? What could you do to change?
- In your journal, consider the questions from page 310. What is your passion? What do you want your life to be about? If you long for something that makes you feel fully alive and part of something specific God is doing for the greater good, ask Him to nurture that vision in you.

Moving past Our Fears into Trust

> *Trust in the LORD with all your heart and lean not on your own understanding; in all your ways submit to him, and he will make your paths straight.*

PROVERBS 3:5-6

WARM-UP

Go around the room and have each woman choose one of the following questions to answer briefly:

What hobbies do you enjoy?

Which do you prefer: the ocean, the mountains, or the forest? Why?

How has a friend encouraged you this week?

After everyone has had a chance to share, open your discussion time with this question:

On a scale of 1 to 10 (1 being almost none, 10 being over the top), how big a part has fear played in your life?

_____

_____

_____

_____

THIS WEEK'S FOCUS

To realize that trusting God is the only solution to fear, and to reflect on the progress we've made in the journey from insecurity to security.

BEFORE YOU MEET

Before your group meets, read chapters 17 and 18 of *So Long, Insecurity.* As you read, highlight or underline parts that jump out to you. What rings true to you? What surprises you? What seems most challenging?

A WORD FROM BETH

{Note to the leader: You might want to read the following aloud to the group.}

You've done it! You've persevered through this study. I am so proud of each of you for tackling your struggles with insecurity head-on. No one knows better than I do how ugly and difficult this journey out of the pit can be. But no one knows better than I do how far God can take us, how much He can transform us, and just how worthwhile the struggle is.

Before we wrap things up, we're going to hit one more big issue: fear. For many of us, it's been a debilitating part of our lives. When we have an insecurity attack, it's a sure bet that fear is behind it. We might be afraid of looking stupid, of being rejected, of being alone, of being betrayed, of being insignificant, of being hurt, or of being disrespected—and that's just the start of the list. There's no getting away from the fact that the world can be a scary place.

But hear this: God is bigger than our fears. Jesus said, "In this world you will have trouble. But take heart! I have overcome the world" (John 16:33). We know that He has overcome the world. Now we have to get that knowledge from our heads to our hearts. We have to learn to trust Him.

DIGGING IN

The bottom line to dealing with insecurity is this: trust God.

> I'm not talking about trusting your man in the middle of that wave of insecurity, although I deeply hope you can and do. I'm talking about something much less reliant on frail flesh and blood: trusting God. Trusting God *with yourself. With your husband. With your job. With your health. With your family. With your friends. With your threat.* I'm talking about entering into a transforming, two-sentence dialogue with a very real, very active God who sees all things and is intimately acquainted with everything concerning you:

You: "Lord, I don't know if I can trust

_____ or not."

God: "But can you trust *Me*?" (pp. 321–322)

How does trusting God differ from trusting a spouse or a set of circumstances?

_____

_____

_____

_____

_____

When we're contemplating all the things that terrify us, the things that strike fear into our hearts in the middle of the night and trigger all our insecurities, we would love a guarantee that those fears will never come true. We desperately want a promise that God will supernaturally protect us from sorrow, so we sometimes try to make God into a divine insurance policy. But that's not the way He works.

I used to think that the essence of trusting God was trusting that He wouldn't allow my fears to become realities. Without realizing it, I mostly trusted God to do what I told Him. If He didn't, I was thrown for a total loop. Over more time than should have been necessary, a couple of realizations finally dawned on me about this thing I was calling trust: (1) It wasn't the real thing. (2) It constantly failed to treat the core issue. Trusting God to never let our fears come to fruition doesn't get to the bottom of where insecurity lurks. It's too conditional. . . .

In order to plant our feet on solid ground, we can drop the conditions off of our trust and determine that God will take care of us *no matter what*. (pp. 323–325)

Have you ever "trusted" God to do what *you* told Him? What was the outcome of that situation?

_____

_____

_____

_____

_____

*What do you think trusting God really looks like?

_____

_____

_____

_____

_____

On pages 327–328 I tell about a time when God prompted me to think through some of my deepest fears. What if they came to pass? What would happen then?

> He and I both knew what I would do. I would be devastated at first. I would probably sin in my anger and say all sorts of things and act all sorts of ways I would live to regret. I would feel inexpressibly lonely and rejected and probably old and ugly. But I knew that finally I'd go facedown before God just as I have a hundred other hard times, accept His grace and mercy, believe Him to take up my cause and work it together for good, and then I would get up and choose to live.
>
> The excruciating emotional exercise was the best thing God ever could have asked from me. He knew I had pictured the devastation and defeat over and over, but I had never gotten any further than that in my imagination. It was as if He said, "As long as you're going to borrow

trouble on the future, why don't you just go ahead and borrow the grace to go with it and see yourself back up on your feet defying your enemy's odds . . . just as you and I have done a dozen other times." (pp. 327–328)

*What do you think would happen if your own worst fears became reality? Why does fear lose its power when we picture God with us on the other side of our tragedies?

_____

_____

_____

_____

_____

This idea gets right to the heart of what God has promised us as believers. Is His highest goal for us a life free of struggle? Hardly. He's our heavenly Father, after all. No parent wants to see his or her child in pain, yet no good parent makes the avoidance of pain the primary focus of child rearing. A child who never experienced pain or frustration would be self-absorbed and spineless—and that's certainly not what God wants for us. But He has promised that nothing will utterly destroy us. Nothing will separate us from Him. No pain or devastation will be wasted; He can turn everything to our good and His glory.

God has promised that His grace will be given according to our need and that not only will we survive by the skin of our teeth, if we trust Him and hang on to Him for dear life—grieving, yes, but as those who have hope—we will also thrive again. We can give ourselves to something greater than painlessness. We can give ourselves to *purpose.* If we cooperate, good will indeed come to us and others around us, and glory will most assuredly come to God. (p. 329)

Have you ever seen God bring good out of pain—either in your life or in someone else's?

_____

_____

_____

_____

_____

I remain confident of this: I will see the goodness of the LORD in the land of the living. Wait for the LORD; be strong and take heart and wait for the LORD. (Psalm 27:13-14)

In chapter 17 we look at Psalm 112:7-8. I've changed the pronouns to reflect the women reading this book: "[She] will have no fear of bad news; [her] heart is steadfast, trusting in the LORD. [Her] heart is secure, [she] will have no fear; in the end [she] will look in triumph on [her] foes."

> She doesn't live in fear of bad news. Why is she free from such self-torment? Stay with me here, because this connection is crucial: she is free because she knows that "in the end [she] will look in triumph on [her] foes." Translation? God will work all things—no matter how difficult or devastating—out to her advantage. Her enemy will not triumph over her. It may hurt in the beginning, but it's going to be beautiful "in the end." (p. 331)

How is it possible not to live in fear of bad news? What do you think it means to "look in triumph" on our foes?

_____

_____

_____

_____

_____

Insecurity feeds like a starving wolf off fear of the future—and not just the distant future of aging, infirmity, or death. Insecurity fears what might happen later today.

Tonight. Tomorrow. Next week. Next year. Next decade. Its constant mantra is, "What will I do if . . . ?" Fear of the future makes people settle for things in the present that completely defy abundant life. It also insults the grace of God that will be piled in heaps for us when hardship comes. We agonize over how we'll possibly make it, yet all the while we can glance over our shoulders and see where God has carried us. And often through worse than what we're afraid of now.

When you feel that familiar panic begin to rise in your heart like a river coursing its banks and your soul begins to roll with another round of "What will I do if . . . ?" what would happen if you were willing to hear the voice of God whisper these inaudible words?

Child, you are asking the wrong question. Here's the one that would assuage your fears: What will God do if . . . ?
(pp. 332–333)

*How would your life change if you stopped asking, "What will I do if . . . ?" and started asking "What will God do if . . . ?"

_____

_____

_____

_____

_____

*What are some things that God promises us? (See page 333.) Which of these promises are especially meaningful for you as you face your fears?

_____

_____

_____

_____

_____

IN THE LIGHT OF THE WORD

Scripture can be a powerful antidote to fear. Let's look at a few passages that call us to have courage and put our trust in the Lord.

*Read Psalm 27:1-6. According to this passage, why don't we need to fear?

_____

_____

_____

_____

_____

*What does David, the writer of this psalm, set forth as his ultimate desire? (See verse 4.)

_____

_____

_____

_____

_____

Verse 4 presents a beautiful picture of intimacy with God—living close to Him, gazing on Him, seeking Him, and finding Him. That's what David really wanted. And I think that's the basis for David's conclusion at the end of the psalm: "I remain confident of this: I will see the goodness of the LORD in the land of the living" (Psalm 27:13). When David lived in close communion with God, he saw God's goodness. David's outward circumstances might not have changed, but his eyes were opened to God's beauty, and he rejoiced in God's presence with him. David learned to trust the Lord, and in doing so, he was able to let go of his fears.

*Read Psalm 46:1-3. What strikes you about the psalmist's trust in God in this passage?

_____

_____

_____

_____

_____

God is our refuge and strength, an ever-present help in trouble. Therefore we will not fear. (Psalm 46:1-2)

*Where does the psalmist's comfort come from?

_____

_____

_____

_____

_____

_____

God's constant presence, God's identity and authority, God's role as our refuge

May we always know that the Lord Almighty is with us and that the God of Jacob is our fortress. No matter what happens in our lives—even if the whole world seems to be falling down around us—may we know that the Lord is God. He will be exalted. He is worthy of our praise, and He is worthy of our trust. Fear not!

WRAP-UP
*At the end of chapter 18 I write that my goal at the conclusion of this journey is to cease being motivated to thought or action in any way by insecurity. What is your goal as you finish this study?

_____

_____

_____

_____

_____

My fervent prayer for all the women in this group is that God has worked mightily in your lives. May you continue to challenge each other, strengthen each other, and build each other up as you rest ever more solidly in the security Christ has given you.

*What has God done in your life through this book or through this group experience? Where would you like to go from here?

_____

_____

_____

_____

_____

Read aloud the prayer on page 346. Then end with additional prayer time for the women in your group, thanking God for the time you have spent together as a community discussing this important topic. Ask God to continue to bring healing, transformation, and renewal in your journey toward security.

ON YOUR OWN

- Reread the list of God's promises (see page 333), and look up the Scriptures indicated. Ask God to help you understand and believe these promises.
- Reread your journal entry from week 1, where you wrote about what you wanted to get out of this study and how you wanted to be changed. Has the group experience met your expectations? Prayerfully consider what new goals you want to set as you finish the group time and move forward from here.